Daily Zen
Charlie Ambler

© Charlie Ambler 2016
ISBN: 9781520189451

Introduction

I started Daily Zen in 2008 to share quotes pertaining to my meditation practice and self-directed studies of Eastern philosophy. Twitter had just started and it seemed like a clever outlet for the aphoristic wisdom I found in various spiritual texts. I didn't expect the project to have an audience of nearly 300,000 after just a few years! I regularly get emails from people who say that my writings have encouraged them through difficult times or changed their perspective on something. This is a great gift. I do not claim to be a Zen master or 'enlightened' by any means. I believe enlightenment is found in each moment we spend in meditation. The community that's developed around Daily Zen has helped me grow and recognize the universality of this mindset. I consider myself the student here.

We all want guidance. When we communicate and listen closely, we find it. Since 2008, I have written thousands of pages, read countless spiritual texts, and maintained my daily meditation practice. The goal of these writings is simply to share my reflections with others. I hope you find something useful in these short essays and that they help you commit further to your meditation practice. If you don't meditate, I hope they encourage you to start.

—*Charlie Ambler*

A Brief Guide to Zen Meditation

Zazen is the practice of Zen meditation. It is an all-encompassing practice and encourages us to remain centered and to stop obsessing over results. It is the connection between you and the present moment. Doing it without expectations cultivates heightened awareness and compassion for others.

Meditating regularly develops a mental process that carries into everyday life. The old saying goes, "When eating, eat. When sitting, sit." Meditation incites a mindfulness that allows us to focus on each tiny breath and moment throughout the day. You already breathe all day long, and so soon this unconscious skill of calm breath acknowledgement carries into every activity you do. You start to meditate all day long without even realizing it, centering your mind with every action. You do the dishes, mindful of scraping every bit of dirt steadily and deliberately. You pet your cat and can enjoy the experience of doing so fully. You work and focus on the task at hand rather than the payoff.

Meditation has taught me to recognize details and to be hyper-observant. Cleaning my room becomes a playful act. So does any other chore. Interactions become more intimate and full of curiosity. This change in mindset can be overwhelming at first.

How do we reconcile finally seeing the world as it is, with all its intrigue? The meditative mind teaches us not to judge. In not judging, everything becomes interesting. This makes being bored a near impossibility. Boredom is simply out of the question for the disciplined meditator. Every activity becomes a reflection of the Zen mind rather than a mere activity. At the very least, boredom becomes an opportunity to return to mindfulness and gratitude.

Meditation allows us to rearrange the entire mental fabric of living. This makes perfect sense, since it's been proven to change the brain chemistry of regular practitioners. The mind is able to recalibrate itself and focus on what really matters: the present. Within the present are the solutions to all problems.

Instead of meditating to become better at your job, rid yourself of addiction, or solve some sort of problem in your life, meditate to meditate. The act of meditating every day will carry over into everything else you do. Doing it for its own sake detaches you from reward- seeking behaviors and attachments. People find themselves magically quitting smoking, drinking less, fighting less and feeling less anxious after even just a few weeks of regular meditation. It's not a miracle; you're just giving your mind some time to decompress.

Let go or be dragged.

"You do not suffer because things are impermanent. You suffer because things are impermanent and you think they are permanent."
— *Thich Nhat Hanh*

Next time you feel upset, zoom out. What are you upset about? Why are you upset about what you are upset about? Keep this train of thought rolling. You'll soon find that there isn't really any reason to be upset other than that you think you should be upset— but you don't want to be upset! So why are you upset?

I use this pattern of deconstruction to help me let go of anger and other irrational emotions. Like everyone else, I often fall victim to such emotions. They are harmful precisely because they consume us and make us forget that we are acting senselessly. We do stupid things, the emotions subside, our rationality returns, and we assess ourselves with regret and embarrassment. Instead of getting frustrated or pushing these emotions away, we should let them wash over us in the same way we let thoughts come and go during meditation.

Rash reactions can be prevented simply by developing the mental discipline to overlap the outburst with the reflection. If you can catch yourself in the moment and simply stop, instead of doing so afterwards, the snowball melts instead of growing larger. This is really difficult for some people, either because of lifelong conditioning or because of deep-rooted feelings of insecurity (or both). We indulge in envy, pity, insecurity, anger, and other self-defeating emotions because they serve as a security blanket. You can always rely on being bummed out. Tearing yourself down is easier than building yourself up. It's easy to do.

Harder, though, is cultivating the self-respect required to be honest to yourself and others without experiencing shock or giving up on mindfulness. Most of our negative emotional states come from an inability to let go of our delusions about who we think we are and what we think is right. If you are too certain about what you believe, you will do stupid things in order to defend your intelligence. You will hurt other people just to make yourself feel even a little bit better. What's the point? We can recognize these actions as destructive when we step back and breathe.

The ego is what tells us to hold on, to not acknowledge that we are wrong, and to continue fighting despite our better judgment. This goes for everyone. All people have weaknesses and parts of their personalities that they lie to themselves about. When they have to think about them, they either lash out or shut down. But when we confront our insecurities and overcome them, these integral facets of ourselves no longer bother us. We grow through confrontation and reflection, not through submission. We learn to work with what we've got rather than wearing a mask of fantasy and delusion.

The key to negating this submissively egoistic attitude is to embody honesty in your own life. It may be difficult at first. You may have to confront parts of yourself that you don't like. But if those parts of yourself are here to stay, why not work with them? Denying them will only make them more harmful to you and your loved ones. As Jung said, "What you resist persists." You may accidentally hurt other people by being honest. But if you help someone struggle through finally being able to understand themselves better, assuming you are compassionate and smart about it, aren't you doing a kind thing?

Compassion does not mean being mindlessly nice to everyone just so they're nice to you back. It means trying to genuinely understand life and to feel empathy. You cannot feel empathy when you lie to yourself and others about your true feelings. You can't sugar-coat the truth, because then it ceases to be the truth. The way of mindfulness requires us to let go of these attachments. We should be compassionate through honesty and confidence and not be scared to say what we feel.

Don't worry about progress.

The cult of progress is everywhere. Science continues to plod ahead at ever-intensifying rates. Technologies develop faster than most people can possibly take the time to understand them. Politicians rely on false conceptions of "change" and "moving forward" to secure a place among the hearts of simple-minded common people willing to cling to anything to feel less suffocated. Welcome to the progress of our age: *material* progress. What you see is what you get. Anything more is 'unobservable'. What place does spirituality have in such a world?

This ideology of material progress strongly relies on a dissatisfaction with the present. It is thus the philosophical credo of perpetual unrest and unhappiness. If we cannot be peaceful and mindful in the present, we certainly can't be peaceful and mindful in the future! This is the modern world's false tenet:

"Right now is unpleasant, so if we move forward, things will get better. The doctrine says, "All we have to do is speed everything up, make more jobs, more technologies, more scientific advances, more money, more of everything. Then everything will be ok."

This is metaphorically comparable to the socially estranged and spiritually bankrupt billionaire sitting alone in his fancy mansion of gold and gadgets and going, "If only I had more gold and gadgets. Then I'd be happy."

True progress eludes humanity since we have deluded ourselves and others into believing that human history is determined by material circumstances. The cult of historical materialism has led humans to believe that religion and spirituality are disposable tools used to achieve tangible goals, not intuitive natural tools for cultivating behaviors that give life meaning: humility, love, loyalty, awe, and self-discipline. Matters of heart and spirit have been neglected in favor of appearances; they are perceived as secondary to the outrageous notion of *external* progress. Even the ancient tradition of meditation practice has been warped by the modern mentality as a tool for efficiency.

The issue here is that when we think of the material world as the most important indicator of progress, we allow materialism to progress *at the expense* of spirituality. We rely on our senses more than ever, neglecting the extra-sensory metaphysical world of spiritual intuition and natural force. Thus, we only recognize what we can experience on a sensory level. Deeper matters, the truly important stuff, remain covered by layers of sensory stimulation and rhetoric.

The result of all this? People become groomed by default to be dissatisfied with life *no matter what*, since they begin to equate the *stuff* of life with life itself. They don't reflect and they don't look within. And what do we have today? A massive world population of technologically advanced people terrified of death, whose spirituality has decayed to such a degree that they *can't* stop to reflect. Real spiritual discipline is terrifying to decadent 21st-century technophiles.

Let us work together to revise the false march towards material progress— a march towards a cliff's edge. Instead, let's direct our attention inward, cultivating the values of spirituality as they have always been cultivated by thoughtful humans. This is about looking into yourself and not attaching to anyone else's ideas. Instead of speed, efficiency, disruption, and material optimization, let us reorient our values towards compassion, mindfulness, gratitude, honesty, and discipline. All that is required is a balance. Right now, the balance skews towards material progress. If we can collectively begin a push towards real internal spiritual growth, we can correct this path.

Let Yourself Go

"The great man, through his actions, will not set out to harm others, nor make much of benevolence and charity; he does not make any move for gain, nor consider the servant at the gate as lowly; he will not barter for property and riches, nor does he make much of his having turned them down; he asks for no one's help, nor does he make much of his own self-reliance, nor despise the greedy and mean; he does not follow the crowd, nor does he make much of being so different; he comes behind the crowd, but does not make much of those who get ahead through flattery. The titles and honors of this world are of no interest to him, nor is he concerned at the disgrace of punishments. He knows there is no distinction between right and wrong, nor between great and little. I have heard it said, "The Tao man earns no reputation, perfect Virtue is not followed, the great man is self-less." In perfection, this is the path he follows."
— Chuang Tzu

As soon as someone starts talking about universal peace, I get skeptical. It's no coincidence that these people are often unpleasant or un-peaceful in their personal lives. I think of someone like John Lennon, who preached a vague notion of peace to the masses but by many accounts sounds like he was a bit of a Machiavellian sadist in his personal life. What people lack internally they often project.

Like most political proclamations, trying to promote universal peace is oddly paradoxical. It means that you are taking time you could be directing towards finding peace within yourself and spending it trying to reframe the world in your image. The irony of humans trying to act like gods in this way is that they often don't even cultivate an image to begin with. Politics and religion are used by many to pretend to be of a certain image rather than as deep catalysts for growth or understanding. Trying to be the change you wish to see in the world when you don't know who you are is contradictory.

I love this lengthy passage from the Taoist master Chuang Tzu; it elucidates the importance of discovering a balance between reflection and projection. Those who preach are often so focused on preaching that they are unable to embody what they preach. I find myself occasionally falling into this problem, and try to make sure that I don't tell people to do anything that I am not willing nor able to do myself. Everyone can be an asshole sometimes, but the key is recognizing when you fall short, accepting yourself, and working to be more mindful. Ideology is not the solution. Mindfulness is, and it's easy— it just requires a willingness to make mistakes and learn from them.

Following this train of thought, the way towards peace is not through politics. Thousands of years of human civilization have made this perfectly clear. To think that the dust is going to suddenly settle once we find the right blanket ideology is wishful thinking that borders on psychosis. The 20th century was proof that mass ideology often does little more than hurt lots and lots of people. The lesson is not in politics *out there*, but in yourself.

If every individual decided to meditate for 20 minutes a day, a heightened degree of peace in the world could be guaranteed. Individualism is only beneficial if people use it to recognize that they can *shed* their sense of self. Selflessness is not being outwardly charitable, but instead cultivating a lack of desire within yourself and a lack of attachment to false notions of self. Those who desire change are often not at peace with themselves.

There can be no peace without peaceful individuals, so the place to start is obvious. This seems so simple and yet people lose sight of the forest for the trees. I'm not sure why this happens, but I believe it is the result of too much trust in culture and appearances. The vanity of concepts convinces people that there is an easy cure to what ails them. Instead of actually taking the steps to find contentment, they distract themselves with quick fixes that don't actually fix anything. It's a very strange pattern of behavior, but it seems to occur in all humans, regardless of circumstance.

Take small steps each day to cultivate peace and non-attachment in your life. People who follow me on Twitter are always making excuses when I say to do this. They say facetiously, "How will I survive if I have no attachments?" This is belligerence. You will find everything you need and maybe even some unforeseen luxury if you learn to let go and simply do what has to be done. The luxury of mindfulness is feeling grateful just for being alive where you are right now. Attaching yourself to concepts like peace, fortune or fame will do nothing but prevent you from feeling at peace. The key is to reflect, quietly, with no desire for attention or recognition. Peace will follow.

Replacing the Profit Motive

I like the term "MO", modus operandi. *Method of operation.* I sometimes picture the brain as possessing a little switch, like a knob on a guitar's distortion pedal. At this point in history, it seems that a large number of people have their delusion pedal switch turn to the PROFIT notch. Not any sort of abstract profit reigns, just simple materialistic monetary profit. From that particular motivation stems a vast array of nuanced implications and actions. There are a few rungs of implications, which can be ascertained by asking yourself the following questions. I've found these questions particularly useful in curbing my own use of the profit motive as the spur behind my actions.

What am I doing for money?
What am I doing in order to do those things?
What am I using money for?
What would I do if money was no object?

Now, the goal here is not some silly utopian vision of a world without aspiration. We all need money, of course, and everyone finds different ways of acquiring it. The purpose in asking yourself that question is to reach a certain degree of honesty with yourself. How much of your day-to-day passions are aligned with the pursuit of material security? Since most of us are not super rich, and most of us have no choice but to worry about money *sometimes*, the answer is usually "a lot".

Understanding how you would spend your time if you didn't spend so much of it acquiring goods and services helps us to recognize the dissonance between thought and action that this world of ours cultivates. Tropes like "don't quit your day job" incite nervous chuckles or condescension. This is rooted in a certain fear innate in large populations of average people that they were not born with the skills required to be truly free in an otherwise free society. In actuality, the most difficult part of becoming financially independent (or accomplishing anything out of the mediocre ordinary) is usually getting over this fear of failure.

The pursuit of profit as a common cultural narrative has completely screwed up our view of what money is for. We trade time for money, which we trade for things that save us time, or make our time more entertaining. If we had more free time, we wouldn't need most of the things we spend money on. This is simplistic but you get the idea. As such, we've come to equate time and money. The more time we trade for money, the more trapped we become.

Equating time and money does an obvious but horror-inducing thing to the brain: it convinces it that a *lack* of money means a *lack* of time, also known as "death". Sometimes it does, sure, but humans have a remarkable endurance. Modernity doesn't give the human capacity for survival and optimization enough credit. I don't think anyone can say the phrase, "If I quit my day job, I will die," honestly. And yet we often feel stuck in places we don't want to be just out of security. This is the source of my Zen humanism: placed in a situation of scarcity or discomfort, a human will usually figure out a way to deal with it. The problem is getting them to *commit*.

Most of us never put ourselves in situations of scarcity or discomfort. We fear a lack of money, a lack of time, a lack of security. And we're all *really* comfortable these days, so people rarely ever take the plunge or take calculated risks that allow themselves to transcend the banality of circumstance and get to know themselves. This is why it's so important to ask yourself what you really want, because what you really want is probably not money. Once the fear of loss is removed from the equation, you can take active steps towards a life of higher risk. You can test your spirit's capacity for innovation, problem-solving, and optimization. This is a motive I can get behind— a spiritual profit motive. Instead of optimizing for financial profit, we optimize for spiritual growth. This occurs through taking optimized risks, cultivating mindfulness, and confronting fears.

The self-discovery from these opportunities and activities makes us into more peaceful people, who are in turn more likely to optimize other parts of life and thus live better, rather than just make a better living. Look at the satisfied self-made people— artists, entrepreneurs, and innovators alike, the ones who are actually contented— the vast majority of them didn't just get lucky. They took risks and used the skills and resources at their disposal to engage with life in a meaningful way. You get the idea— profit should come as a reward for living a brave and virtuous life, not the other way around.

Using this methodology, it isn't hard to explain why there are so many unhappy people scurrying around trying to hoard all the gold. It isn't hard to explain why so many comfortable upper-middle class people are depressed, anxious, and addicted to food, drugs and alcohol. It isn't hard to explain why vapid sources of entertainment exist in spades, while libraries and institutions of higher learning are being hollowed of value from the inside-out. Many modern people have forgotten what it means to be human— to subject ourselves to risks, fears, and problems, and emerge from the flames with a heightened sense of self and a new understanding of life.

Unhappiness & Mindfulness

In the usual narratives people read in books, watch on TV and subsequently rehearse over and over in their heads, life happens to an external figure that they subsequently identify with.

The protagonist exists.
The world happens to them.
They choose to react.

It's a cause-and-effect relationship. This is how storytelling works, since it's something "out there". It's something people usually absorb rather than produce. Once they start projecting themselves onto such narratives, a weird transference occurs. The projection becomes the person. People view themselves as characters acting on a stage. It's why they dress up in different costumes, call themselves by different labels, and associate with different people. You can move to a city and pretend to be anyone if you get the image down properly. And you likely won't ever be questioned for it. Everything is permitted, and yes, such a gigantic revolution in the realm of "identity politics" has not left us immune to huge consequences.

The more prevalent this obsession with archetypes and images has become, the more people project themselves onto the images. It's why fashion is so popular and the turnover rate for trends is so high.

It's why celebrities can't just be people who do their jobs well — they have to be that *plus* post-human sex icons, like vain ancient gods and goddesses. Sometimes they can get really far by *just* being post-human sex icons. They are required by audiences and cultural engineers alike to represent archetypes of human extremity at their most primal. This heightens the narrative's power and makes it more sensational.

Crowds respond well to sensation. It's why billions watch superhero movies and only a comparative few watch boring 3-hour long existential French new wave movies. It's why most radio stations play top-40 and not weird hip noise music. People prefer the simple and reliable to the complex and dynamic. Why? The simple and reliable are *better,* as far as our general instincts are concerned. Doritos taste better than celery because, unlike celery, Doritos are scientifically engineered to appeal to humans. Nature doesn't care about our preferences; culture *does* and profits from them.

The narratives we form in our heads about ourselves and others follow the same simplicity— they become unnaturally engineered in favor of gratifying base human instinct. The actor of the self becomes the character. The more this character rehearses its carefully crafted subconscious script, the further away a person moves from their actual self, and the more spiritual work they have to do to return to the true self. This is often determined simply by circumstance. It's not something most people reflect on much. If they did, the modern world would look a lot different.

For this reason, reflection has become tantamount to retaining a connection to the natural self and the natural world. As reality blends further into virtuality, the real is becoming more difficult to discern. Spiritual crises abound. People have been telling themselves false narratives about themselves for so long that they cannot discern between "the matrix" and real life. It is no coincidence that a cultural aversion to real confrontation and honesty has emerged alongside modern humanity's insanely complicated web of imagined personalities.

This is where meditation inevitably enters the picture. For a person who spends thousands of hours looking at screens, projections, and images, both in real life and in the mind's eye, closing the eyes and sitting down in a quiet place for any length of time is antithetical to their animal instinct. Why not subject oneself to more sensation and distraction 24/7? The reason is pretty simple: overexposure to the instant gratification of image culture leads people to hold themselves to standards that, because they appeal so heavily to animal instincts, are entirely unsustainable to us as evolved human. As a result, the ego projections made by most people leave them deeply unhappy and thirsting for something else. That something else is usually sold to them in the form of a potentially remedial product, which obviously don't work for long, since trying to cover up identity crises with consumer goods is like putting a band-aid on a bullet wound.

What appeals to us in fantasy appeals to us precisely because it *cannot* be achieved in reality. Those who do achieve their fantasies find them to be drastically less amazing than their mind had predicted in a time of scarcity. The human mind adjusts to whatever it's exposed to and sets new standards. This spurs people to action, but many of these actions are in vain.

Meditative practice helps all this mental dust settle. Over time, it helps us discern mindfully between the fantasy and the real, self and other, ego and non-ego, projection and reality, etc. Most people are buried under layers and layers of false projections, either consciously performed or just stuck in limbo as a result of never being noticed. Once they get noticed, they shift around. Real honest truths, which are often subtle, personal, and difficult to translate into word, emerge. Actions subsequently shift in a similarly nuanced (but still transformative) way. The cycle gets going, thought and action informing one another cyclically until a person's entire life begins to change.

Becoming Yourself

Many people do not have enough time to become themselves. They fill their time with work, relationships and hobbies that distract them from boredom and bad feelings. They live fast-paced lives designed to disallow the periods of reflection that would render their way of living unnecessary or wasteful. They live as most of us live— doing the best they can with what they have, but often unaware of the deeper implications of their thoughts and actions on their sense of well-being. What happens when you only look 'out there' for truth? What happens if you never look within?

The simple answer is that the truth never quite arrives. You end up living life staring through a false projection of reality and die never having experienced the world outside of your limited purview. In this regard, meditation is indeed a wonderful activity; it gives you direct access to inner truth regardless of your past, background or place in the world. It allows you to grow into yourself, regardless of who you are or who you think you are.

If you never take time to reflect, you end up inhabiting a world of pure illusion. Thoughts, emotions and external stimuli control your thoughts and actions. You may find yourself a slave to money, sex, power and other attachments. You may find yourself wanting to be someone else, behaving like someone else, and believing yourself to be someone who you are not. Our chaotic world of images has countless emerging consequences that we won't recognize until history shifts its tides back away from our narcissism.

In looking within, you discover that you have pretty much everything you need. You are the source of all your happiness, sadness, failure and success. These judgments do not exist in the external world but are projected onto it by your ego and cultural influences. One man's trash is another man's treasure. Judgment upon the external world comes from within; controlling it changes your world, sort-of like a software update. If your mind is uncontrolled and indulgent, you end up living in a bugged state of delusion. You waste energy to function at a sub-optimal level.

Some people begin meditating and are shocked by how a genuine this new understanding of the self feels. For this reason, meditation can be dangerous. If you've spent years and years dwelling under countless layers of delusions, false judgments and vain motivations, meditation might really mess with your head. Is this a red pill that you're willing to swallow? For me, the answer has always been yes. It is always better to suffer over the truth of reality (adaptation) than to suffer over your delusional interpretations of reality (stagnation).

Through the former, we forge a new perspective with new possibilities. Through the latter, we remain stuck in the cycle of everyday samsara.

Saying yes to true understanding is often a difficult path. Pretty much everyone you meet and everything you see, especially if you live in an apex of modern life like a city or a university, serves the interest of projected false realities. Dishonesty has always run rampant in human common life because fantasy, solipsism and idealization are easier than true reflection. Spiritual truths cannot be packaged or sold; they come from self discovery.

Similarly, with so many technological distractions and a total lack of societal control over impulses, decadence becomes a norm rather than a vice. Overindulgence in food, drugs, sex and ideology are the norm rather than the exception. Without restraints or standards or reflections, there are no honest questions. Without these questions, we lose our way and forget the true path.

For this reason, to be a daily meditator in 2016 is a profoundly self-directed and even revolutionary act. That is not to say that it will turn you into an ideologue or a revolutionary. It will do the opposite— turn you into a self-confident and honest person in a world full of weakness, clinging and indulgence. Meditation reveals yourself to you.

The Art of Gratitude

"A wise man will leave the gold in the mountain and the pearls to lie in the deep. He does not view money and goods as true profit, nor is he attracted by fame and fortune, nor by enjoyment of long life, nor sadness at an early death; he does not value wealth as a blessing, nor is he ashamed by poverty. He will not lust for the wealth of a generation to have as his own; he has no wish to rule the whole world as his private domain. His honor is clarity of understanding that all life are part of one treasury and that death and birth are united." —Chuang Tzu

The distractions of the world tempt many a good person every day. People are sucked up by desire—they yearn for wealth, freedom, happiness and fame. In yearning, they neglect the present. When you want something badly enough, attaining it will not satisfy your need. This is a sad paradox, but we must not despair. We have the ability to transcend it through awareness.

In wanting, people prevent themselves from feeling future contentment. This is because their contentment is given a condition. Once that condition is met, they believe contentment will follow. But how can a mind that is trained to feel desire more often than contentment end up feeling contentment more often? It's a non sequitur. The mind that trains itself to desire *more* will be stuck in the cycle of having *less*. It's better that people skip the desire and focus on the contentment.

This means cultivating gratitude. It means recognizing what one has and understanding that yes, it is enough. Why it is enough? It's enough precisely because choosing the path of attachment means that nothing will *ever* be enough. When you bet your contentment on future rewards, you inhibit yourself from that contentment. Better to choose the path of non-attachment and be pleasantly surprised by your blessings.

People can distract themselves as much as they want with shiny things, goals, fame and achievements, but the yearning that causes such a desire for distraction can't be addressed if you aren't honest with yourself. Self-honesty allows the truth to come through. Simply ask yourself lots of questions. Get to the bottom of why you yearn so deeply for what you yearn for. Why do you want what you want? Why do you do what you do?

It's OK to search, but only for the sake of searching. Lose your ego in the act of doing and living rather than trading the present moment for a future promise. Searching for things outside yourself without recognizing the infinitude of the moment will lead you astray. You'll feel perpetually stuck in the cycle of desire. Everyone is a part of this cycle, but those who reflect and know to be grateful prevent themselves from getting sucked into it too deeply. There's always time to shift your perspective towards appreciation.

Remind yourself of what you cherish in life every day. Recognize that the you that has a billion dollars or a soulmate is the same you that you are right now. No external circumstances can change who you are; you are responsible for yourself. Reflect on this innate sense of purpose. Cope with it. Those who understand that their lot in life is mostly a matter of perspective will find contentment without bankrupting their souls.

Some parting words from Chuang Tzu:

"Be still, be pure, do not make your body struggle, do not disturb your essence. All this will result in a long life. The eye does not see, the ear does not hear, the heart knows nothing, yet your spirit will guard your body and your body will have a long life. Guard what is within, block that which is outside, for much knowledge is dangerous."

Confronting Your Demons

"What, if someday or night a demon were to steal after you into your loneliest loneliness and say to you: 'This life as you now live it and have lived it, you will have to live once more and innumerable times more' Would you not throw yourself down and gnash your teeth and curse the demon who spoke thus? Or have you once experienced a tremendous moment when you would have answered him: 'You are a god and never have I heard anything more divine.'"
— *Friedrich Nietzsche*

Someone I was advising recently said, "I feel my demons are stronger than I am." I couldn't lie to him. I said, "You know what? I think you're right." I've been in the same situation before. For many people, dealing with difficult negative emotions feels overpowering. This is very often a correct assessment; feeling helpless in the face of problems often comes from not cultivating the proper skills needed to confront them. People know deep down that they haven't equipped themselves with the skills needed to deal with certain emotions and events, and they punish themselves for it. Instead of punishing ourselves, though, we can learn to build a stronger mind.

If you want to fight a dragon, you have to arm yourself. You can't go out butt-naked with no armor or weapons and expect to win. To do so would be foolish. Even if you believe in your innate self, there are things you can do to bolster your spiritual strength and awareness. You can't just suddenly decide to triumph over your difficulties in the same way you can't just suddenly decide to become a heavyweight boxer and compete. Cultivating inner-peace requires work, and even when it feels impossible it's always time well-spent.

When you feel your demons are stronger than you, you're probably onto something. If you continue to feel helpless and sorry for yourself, you let the problems get stronger while you stagnate. But if you use this sense of helplessness to cultivate inner-strength and courage, you'll overcome them. The key is to direct this energy inward. Meditate. Exercise. Work on yourself. Build the confidence and gusto required to rise above your mental baggage. Recognize the absurdity of allowing concepts to bring you down. This is one of the core lessons of Zen— what you think is not real. Thoughts are all abstractions. We shouldn't take them so seriously. Latching onto external concepts and feeling disappointed often makes people feel like the world is crumbling in on them. This feeling of dread is truly difficult. But only through conscious work and practice can we overcome it.

There's no magical solution to deeply rooted problems and concerns, but if you do a little work each day to be aware and more present, you eventually find the strength to confront your demons when they come about. This is a lifelong journey and there are always surprise rewards along the way. The key is to stick with it, to practice your most conscious practice every day and not to give up out of disappointment.

The Impact of Meditation

"If you want to conquer the anxiety of life, live in the moment, live in the breath." —Amit Ray

I've been lifting weights for 5 years, which is half as long as I've been meditating. Exercise has changed me more than I would have thought when I started. I have become less anxious and less depressed. I am in better control of my habits. I am more confident. Physically, I am stronger and have more endurance. I can move really heavy things with ease and carry moderately heavy things a fair distance. My skin has improved, my sex life is better, etc, you get the idea. After a good workout, I feel less angry and my mind is sharper. I enjoy all of these benefits and have devoted much thought to why I enjoy them so much— I have let go of wanting to achieve results. What led to this?

Mostly, exercise reconnects you with your body. Many people are disconnected from their bodies and so do not appreciate the other more nuanced benefits of keeping the body active and engaged like the mind. They do not recognize the relationship between mentality and physicality. Fine-tuning the body also sharpens the mind, which in turns enhances your relationship to the world around you. You see clearer, think clearer and feel more empowered to take risks and do things. Not only this, exercise influences your relationship with yourself. You become willing to suffer and work hard to live more fully rather than as means to an end goal. It doesn't always feel good, and that's when it's most important to persevere for your own sense of humility.

Back to Zen mind. No more of this results talk. No more ego talk. Meditation has the same effect on the mind as exercise on the body. Let's think about it analogically. When you do resistance training, you work specific muscle groups really hard. They become exhausted and damaged from working so hard. When the fibers repair, they are stronger. You repeat this as much as you want to grow stronger, bigger, leaner, whatever your goals are. But eventually the visible benefits plateau. What then? The process must become more important than the results. It becomes a meaningful ritual. The process always requires patience because it is mindful rather than delusional. It requires commitment. It requires an ability to suffer not for a goal, but for its own sake.

Anyone who has meditated for a while will tell you that this process applies to meditation in the mental realm. In the beginning, your mind is often very sore. It gets distracted. It fails to stay focused. It experiences intense emotions and thoughts. It loses its way. Sometimes it uncovers painful thoughts and memories that it wanted to hide. With all this suffering and difficulty comes understanding, but only if we make peace with it and endure it. With such non-progressive "progress" comes moments of pure bliss, beauty and awakening. These experiences are impossible without a fair bit of struggle and patience.

I view exercise and meditation as the two most mystical and fascinating practices in this world. I am so grateful I have them in my life. I don't feel attached to them or compulsive. Every day when I meditate I am grateful to have the time and energy to do so. Sometimes it feels rewarding, other times disappointing. If I judged it, I would not be practicing with honesty and dedication. When I go to the gym, I savor every breath I take. I try to eat properly and recover properly. These are not activities that we do to get better at life; they *are* life. Add mindful contemplation into the mix and you can really enhance your relationship with both yourself and the external world. Meditating and exercising with diligence while respecting the lessons of the process provides us with a sense of deep meaning. The connection you develop with yourself— your body, your mind, etc— connects you with the whole world. It helps you recognize the fabric of who you are and also to see yourself as an integral part of the fabric of the world.

Identify with Nothing

"You can't even trade a single fart with the next guy. Each and every one of us has to live out his own life. Don't waste time thinking about who's most talented."
—Kodo Sawaki

The single biggest obstacle in my mindfulness practice is my ego. I have always tried to identify with things outside of myself for my sense of self-worth. I've come to terms with this thanks to my meditation practice, but that doesn't mean it doesn't still creep in. The journey never ceases. So, this is not just about myself but about The Self, and how we obscure a true understanding of the self in favor of more shallow external signifiers.

Culture
For a while I identified strongly with the cultural stuff I liked— music, art, movies, etc. I valued these things not always for their own sake but instead for what their specific virtues signified to others about me, thus identifying with them. Was I just another plebeian who loved 'popular stuff' or did I have a more *refined* sensibility? Was I just a run of the mill Cool Guy or did I have extreme or obscure taste? How would I convey this to others in ways both subtle and tasteful enough to seem organic?

How vain and destructive such thought patterns are in the long term!

This is the trap of cultural intelligence. The hipster or the connoisseur convinces himself that what he likes or loves, including people and ideas, defines him. Not only that— he convinces himself that liking X and not Y makes him *good* and not *bad*. Finally, he denies participating in this sort of egoism vehemently and wonders why he feels unfulfilled! If we want to find true mindfulness, we must start by being honest.

Stuff that is considered culturally 'superior' is often valuable and entertaining, but that doesn't mean we should identify with it. What I found was that I was only capable of truly enjoying life when I let go of this sense of attachment and followed my gut. My tastes have become markedly less cool but I have certainly become more comfortable with who I am and I no longer feel the need to signal to others 'who I am'. Worth it? 100%.

Politics
Like most people of all political persuasions, I grew up never asking any genuinely penetrative ideological questions. I only questioned "the other side"— their character, their intelligence, their motivations. I unconsciously pushed them away so that I could alienate them enough to pretend that

they were 'evil' or 'stupid'. When we convince ourselves that other people are not like us, we can write them off without asking any truly penetrative questions. This is essentially the same as treating people we don't want to understand as objects. When you do this you basically just judge anyone who doesn't think like you as inherently inferior. How sad and egoistic is that? We cannot overcome internal and external conflicts when we participate in them so obviously!

I bought in to our era's uniquely subtle brand of propaganda and social conditioning and I was, of course, as wrong as any other unwitting fundamentalist. I no longer identify with any shallow ism, nor do I hold views inherently appealing to either side of any limited spectrum. Most importantly, I try to keep my actual opinions to myself, lest I be crucified by those who are still caught in the trap of ideology.

Ideological commitment rids you of your humanity over time. No matter how smart you are, as soon as you identify yourself with a specific ideology, your inborn spiritual intelligence stops there. Why? You stop asking questions and start making assumptions. You stop reflecting and start projecting. As soon as I realized that I was forfeiting my brain in order to feel committed to being "the good guy", I quit. I started reading stuff on every end of the spectrum rather than just the stuff that agreed with me. The goal should not be being correct, but being compassionate.

This is how one cultivates real intelligence— by sparing nothing. Sometimes it means staring into the abyss. Other times it means staring into complete nonsense. But it's worth the journey because it jogs you out of your countless layers of individualized conditioning. I now know that every ideological movement in history is united in believing they are doing the right thing. What varies is their definition of what is 'right' and often a fundamental variation in their assumptions. All assumptions are false. We are humans, not gods.

I love escaping these traps. I have enjoyed discovering countless new worlds of thought outside of my cultural conditioning. Exiting the tunnel of ideology has taught me not to identify with my politics, but instead of be completely honest with myself, to read, and to observe.

Achievements
I am quickly learning just how slippery the slope of ambition is. When we yearn for the next accomplishment, we turn ourselves into mindless addicts. We thirst for the next dopamine burst, whether from a new romantic partner, life experience, or business transaction. People lose themselves in these goals because such intimate

goals inevitably become intertwined with the self. As soon as you identify with your achievements, you set yourself up for suffering.

Meditation has helped me detach from my achievements. Ironically, this has led to me achieving more than I had when I was obsessed with success. Instead of thinking I'm hot shit for accomplishing something or thinking I'm a failure for missing the mark, I simply tend to what must be done today. In focusing on the present, the future and past become irrelevant. When I am truly lost in the moment, whether it's writing, cleaning the house, or working, I find myself. This only occurs when I apply the meditative mindset of non-attachment and let things unfold naturally. We lose the ego and uncover the self.

Meditation teaches us not to cling to *anything*. With clinging comes delusion. With delusion comes suffering. All that you can realistically do is focus on what you have to do today. Do it without seeing it as a means to an end or an obligation, but instead as its own form of meditation. With this attitude, life becomes a grand experiment in constant mindfulness.Sometimes we miss the mark, but we never feel like failures because we are unattached to the mark itself. Every 'failure' is a chance to learn, every 'success' a chance to be humble and skeptical. To wrap this all up, I find it useful to contrast these two concepts: losing *yourself* vs. losing your *ego*.

When you're fully engrossed in the moment, you lose your ego and find yourself. When you're always thinking about the next thing and acting and clinging mindlessly, you lose yourself and strengthen your ego. Meditation trains us to let go of the ego.

Discovering Stillness

Stillness is defined by a lack of movement. What is calm and still in nature moves slowly or not at all, with a vastness and consistency that humbles as much as it inspires. I look at the stolid dependability of a tree or a flower and remember that we have much to learn about life from these things that we write off as simple.

As soon as you begin to focus on an object with a certain benign indifference, you'll find life in it. Everything is charged with some sort of energy. I don't mean this in a hippie dippie acid dream sense, but instead in a simple perceptual sense. The energy of a given external stimulus is determined by how you judge it. If you train your attention to be neutral, you uncover unforeseen opportunities and nuances.

Meditation practice challenges us to find this stillness. By willfully exposing ourselves to a lack of movement, we grant ourselves permission to tune into the spontaneous stillness of nature. Finding the stillness is much like zoning into a special frequency. Most of the time we're tuned to a loud and chaotic frequency full of ambitions, desires, judgments and anxieties, but a frequency of meditative stillness exists pervasively beneath all of this. Like darkness, it precedes light. It floats under what we perceive to be reality, and as a result it often reflects deeper truths than what we see on the surface.

My mind always tries to throw off the stillness. This is the specialty of the human; it arrogantly and naively attempts to assert its own subjectivity on an objective and uncaring whole. Nature is the substructure, human projection the superstructure. We build an artificial reality on top of a natural reality that already exists, and thus over time the layers thicken and we become less aware of true reality, causing pain and conflict. Meditation is a truly revelatory act in these times; it helps us slowly return to these natural depths and contemplate what true being is. This is a practice that society as a whole has long forgotten. Reviving it is key to our survival as a species.

Mindfulness, Consistency and You

Getting started is often the most difficult part of any endeavor. The human mind will do anything to procrastinate, especially when it has been trained by distractions and a cultural acceptance of laziness. A few years ago it was discovered that nearly half of all the people who take antidepressants have nothing wrong with them chemically. Having gone through periods of both profound laziness and profound productivity, I can say with assurance that what people sometimes misperceive as depression is often just a sense of purposelessness. A lack of direction makes one feel hopeless, but direction is self-imposed. Boredom fuels hopelessness, which fuels more boredom. In other words, the ball is in your court. Recognizing this is a crucial step in reorienting yourself towards a life of meaning. It is harsh but necessary.

Let's back up for a second. Lao Tzu famously said, "The journey of a thousand miles begins with one step." Details help us focus less on achievement and more on direct action. Some people achieve great things and never feel satisfied. Some people achieve nothing and feel perfectly satisfied. Others achieve great things and feel perfectly satisfied. None of this is important. The key to *doing* is to focus on the details rather than the big picture. Make each step count while detaching yourself from expectations.

How does this relate to the previous paragraph about self-imposed depressive periods? Well, if you haven't trained yourself to be detail-oriented, you likely indulge in a variety of small behaviors that contribute to the feeling of meaninglessness. Contrast the aforementioned anti-depressant statistics with statistics for junk food, TV, porn, masturbation, smoking, drugs, inactivity, video games, illiteracy, and financial irresponsibility and you start to paint a pretty grim picture of a large portion of the modern population. People think they are depressed because they've been led by advertising and marketing to neglect the fine print of life— simplicity. They feel that they have no hope because they exhibit behaviors that communicate that they are OK with feeling narcotized. They take individualism as an excuse to be indulgent and hedonistic rather than controlled and intelligent.

The key to reverse this destructive cycle is mindfulness. It's why meditation has become popular in the West alongside explosions of technological innovation. Meditation wakes people up from this existential slumber. Those who are least disciplined, healthy and happy are often the first ones to jump at the throats of anyone who criticizes their lifestyle. People only become defensive when they recognize truth in what the critic is saying, but feel helpless in the face of this truth. The person who is self-satisfied and confident in the details of their life experiences no ill feelings towards critics. Most of the time they don't even pay attention to critics! They are too busy trying to understand themselves better.

Meditation allows you to receive criticism from the deepest parts of yourself with grace. It allows you to reflect. It lets you recognize your complete freedom in this world, but simultaneously recognize that indulging in whatever you want is not the way towards contentment. It's actually just a path towards more craving. Meditation reminds you that what you perceive as unhappiness with life is often just unhappiness with petty situations. Changing these circumstances can revolutionize your emotional state.

Most importantly, mindfulness teaches us consistency. A thousand miles is roughly 2,000,000 steps. That's a lot of steps. If we think about how many steps that is it makes us want to go drink a whiskey, smoke a cigarette, and bark at the moon. How the hell are we going to make the most of 2,000,000 steps? That's the *indulgent* attitude. The big picture is indulgent. It makes us feel bigger than we are for a second, and then it makes us feel powerless. The mindful attitude is to simply start walking. Thich Nhat Hanh titled one of his books, "Peace is Every Step". Think about that sentence as you go about your day. When you choose peace in a moment of profound distress, you make the most of that step. When you use problems as fuel rather than getting angry, you make the most of that step.

You can never know for certain if you will make it 1,000 miles. We all die. We all get ill. You can't know when it's going to happen. It doesn't really matter. As the masters say, the journey is the destination. The obstacle is the path. In making the most of each step, you cultivate health, knowledge, and consistency through sheer awareness. Every healthy, wise and consistent step builds you up to be a healthier, wiser, and more consistent person. This sounds so simple but it's truly wonderful. The decision to learn, grow and be honest with yourself will help you rise above what you perceive as the meaningless of life. Instead of indulging, you learn to let go.

Meditation and Self-Indulgence

Since I was a little kid, my greatest vice has been my impulsiveness. I tend to overindulge in my vices, whether that means eating sugary foods, oversleeping, or rushing my work. I've spoken to other people about this and find a common thread among many people who meditate— they often begin their spiritual journey as a reaction to their perceived overindulgence and impulsiveness. Those who are drawn intrinsically to self-discipline are often those who need to work hardest at it.

When you really commit to meditation, it completely changes the way you approach life. People who try to commit to meditation with the promise that it will change them often fail to follow through. This is because meditation is hard. It's really hard sometimes, actually. The crux of it is this: meditation is hardest for the people that it is most useful for. What meditation calms in you is the same thing that draws you to it.

This becomes starkly evident in the midst of sitting. Every time I meditate for 20 minutes, my body begins to grow restless 5–10 minutes in. If I am in an indulgent mood, I will stop at 10 minutes. I will feel a certain sense of disappointment with myself when I do this, because I know what happens if I do commit to the full 20 minutes and push past my impulsiveness. If I decide to stick with it, every minute that passes feels shorter as my analytical mind fades into the background. My mind grows clearer and clearer. By the end of the 20 minutes, I feel the powerful mind of no-mind. This self-discipline, if practiced every day, keeps you in check and revolutionizes your life, precisely through detaching you from a desire to be something other than what you are.

In being an impulsive person, the greatest thing I can do for myself is finding controlled practices through which I can exhibit self-discipline. I am drawn to exercise for the same reason. I can do 3 sets at the gym and then leave and go to McDonalds, but that only perpetuates the mental cycle of laziness. You may not realize it, but your deeper subconscious recognizes when you are being lazy and self-indulgent, and you punish yourself for it through a sense of subtle guilt and shame. In cultivating self-discipline, these qualities of guilt and shame transform into a healthily modest sense of self-respect over time.

Whether you're a novice or a seasoned meditator, recognize that the most important part of your practice comes when you want to give up. When you hit initial resistance and want to call it quits, make a point of overcoming this impulse. It can be really hard to do if your mind is distracted and fractured. But let me tell you— pushing past mental resistance during meditation on a regular basis is a powerful act of mindfulness. Sitting through such mental boundaries with a non- clinging mind cultivates an inner-strength, a solid core. I notice it when I devote energy to following through with my meditation.

No one's perfect and everyone encounters various forms of mental resistance throughout the day. In developing self-respect and self-discipline in your daily meditation practice, you make a statement to both yourself and the world at large: you are willing to commit. You're willing to wait through obstacles and do what you can with what you have. Simple as it may be, this is an incredibly powerful message to send to yourself. It will change you, but only if you resign yourself to the process.

What Meditation Does

Zen practice encourages us to ask questions. The typical questions asked are things like, "What is the nature of being?" or, "What is no-mind?" It's false to ask, "What will meditation do for me?"

Judging by the popular answers to this question, we don't live in a world that's embarrassed by practicing meditation for personal gain. In fact, most of the people who practice (or at least those who try to start) do it to improve their lives. This is a natural tendency of humans— to optimize.

Meditation will completely revolutionize your life and make you calmer, happier, and more productive. It will make sex better. It will make exercise easier. The list goes on. Here's the catch though: it will only help you if you let go of these potential benefits. The benefit of meditation is that it detaches us from an obsession with benefits and allows us to be grateful for this very moment. This means not concerning yourself too much with results. I get it— this seems antithetical to the whole point. If we're trying to improve ourselves and the world, why am I telling you not to concern yourself with results? The reason is that things are often best improved by leaving them alone.

Obsessing over results prevents us from devoting adequate energy to the process. There have been countless times when I've written about meditation regularly but not practiced it myself. This mistake itself was a lesson in my practice. We 21st-century dweebs like to talk the talk but it's far rarer for us to consistently walk the walk, day-in and day-out. The secret to really understanding yourself as a meditator is to immerse yourself in the process so diligently that you forget about any results.

People don't realize that the benefits of meditation come from not focusing on the results. Sometimes it takes them years to figure out this sense of no-mind. That's what meditation is— a full overhaul of the mind that shifts our focus from instant rewards to long-term consistent patience. It is anti-thought, in a sense.

Meditation trains the patience muscle. It trains the curiosity muscle. While it trains these, it helps shrink the fear muscle, the vanity muscle, the talking muscle, the delusion muscle, the overachievement muscle. But thinking about the muscles does not train them. Only diligent practice trains them.

When we meditate, we let thoughts appear. We let them float by. And then we let them disappear instead of holding onto them. Think about all of the energy you've wasted by holding onto stale thoughts. We hold onto false assumptions about the world, political ideologies, labels, grudges, and bad habits. Meditation trains the brain to, over time, recognize that these patterns are just projections and do not adequately represent reality. They have only as much power as we give them. As we continue training the mind, we learn its language, which is beyond what we already think of as language. We can then direct the energy we used to waste wallowing in self-pity, hatred, and boredom towards real living.

This is not exaggeration, especially for modern people. A simple ten minutes a day of simple breathing meditation will slowly change your entire mode of perception. You'll find yourself experiencing these benefits all day every day, but only if you are willing to let go. Your mind will wake up from its slumber, a slumber caused by all the noise, sensation and distraction of the modern world. And slowly, you'll rise above vain thoughts about the people around you— just not intentionally. Your mind will be trained not to respond with pride or arrogance; you'll just keep practicing patiently.

That's another great benefit of meditation: it teaches how to deal with benefiting from itself. Everything you need to start you have right now. Sit down, quiet down, and get breathing. Life will become more vivid. You redirect away from clinging and towards gratitude.

Healthy Detachment

One of the skills meditation teaches us most comprehensively is the art of not getting too attached to thoughts, feelings or ideas. People often think of attachment in the material realm— those who seek to rid themselves of attachment might think of this in terms of money, possessions, or even relationships. But non-attachment is more nuanced than this. You don't want to become a cold cyborg who navigates the world with no attachments whatsoever. Doing so would be a forfeiture of your humanity. Sure, it's possible to withdraw completely into the self, but many of our attachments provide us with meaning in the real world. We shouldn't get rid of them just because we think they might cause us suffering. Everything in life is a trade-off.

A degree of attachment occurs whenever you stumble upon something you like. It could be something you find visually appealing, pleases you, or aligns with your perceived goals and purpose in life. Over time, people begin to associate their sense of purpose with the attachments that provide them with that purpose. In the realm of things, they hoard and stockpile money and possessions, believing that these things contribute to their self-worth. In the realm of ideas, they become extremists and ideologues, refusing to entertain new ideas. In the realm of relationships, they become codependent, sexually obsessive or abusive, fearful of losing what they believe to be filling an internal void. With a heightened belief in the importance of external things and ideas comes a fear of losing them. This fear is the part of attachment that causes us to harm ourselves and one another. It prevents self-awareness and love from taking root.

Fear makes us act irrationally. It stokes the emotions like nothing else. Fear provokes us and encourages us to act out, get angry or change our course of action against our intuition or better judgment. To be mindful is to recognize fear when it comes about and to understand why it's unnecessary. There are very few things in this world that we should actually be scared of. There are also very few things that we should feel so attached to that we fear losing them. To attach yourself this much to something sets you up for disappointment no matter what. Recognize who you are with nothing so that you are not terrified of losing what is not part of your true self.

The easiest example of such clinging is the fear of death. How absurd it is that just about everyone on this Earth fears the one thing that is guaranteed in life! Why stop at the initial gut reaction to death? Why recognize that it's inevitable and make peace? This is so simple and yet barely anyone does it.

How many things would you do differently if you weren't fearful of suffering and discomfort, for example? Such a framework of thinking can be applied to other fears and thus can be used to subdue harmful degrees of attachment.

Some examples:

Money
You don't technically own anything. All you have is your body. Everything else is "on loan" from the universe, as the Stoics liked to say. No matter how much money you have, you could lose it all today. You can't take any money with you to the grave. Better to be grateful for what you have rather than overly attached and fearful of losing it. The best way to practice this is to give some of your wealth away to others or to use it mindfully.

Relationships
You can't rely on anyone except yourself. Relationships with other people can be beautiful and provide meaning to life, but when people get too attached they invent dramas and problems. As soon as you fear losing someone, you dehumanize them. Remember: they don't belong to you. No one belongs to anyone. Instead, be grateful for the presence of others in your life while they are around. If you can't feel grateful for these relationships, find new ones that do incite your gratitude. You are never bound to anyone. This will

make your connections rooted in benevolence rather than fear or neediness.

Work

Your job isn't who you are. For all you know, you could be replaced by a robot tomorrow. When you identify with what you do, you get boastful and competitive. Instead of being fearful of losing your job or worried about being replaced, remind yourself that you can do whatever you want with your time. The more you devote yourself to daily mindfulness, the more you appreciate each moment of your time. Time spent worrying about petty problems only disconnects you from the beauty of the moment.

The key, as with just about everything, is moderation and consistency. The goal shouldn't be to eliminate attachment or suffering from your life. What's important is to recognize your attachments and cultivate a healthy relationship with them. Confront fear. Fear is a symptom that there's work to be done. It's an opportunity. Use these opportunities to change and grow as learning experiences. They aren't burdens. Growing past fears and unhealthy attachments uncovers the inherent meaning in life.

Meta-Mindfulness

"The world is won by those who let it go."
—Lao Tzu

Writing provides an excellent precedent for living when done with a certain degree of abandon. I woke up today and didn't particularly feel like writing, but lately I've pledged to write 1000 words a day and I don't plan on letting up on that anytime soon. I had to just let go, sit down, and get to it. Even if I produced nothing of value, what is meaningful is the process itself and the cultivation of mindful habitual action.

Strengthening our daily habits requires a type of mindful mindlessness that is akin to the ancient Chinese concept of Wu Wei. Wu Wei is "non-doing", but is seen in practice as action through inaction. When we act without overthinking, we act most purely. Actions become effortless and organic rather than forced. It's a form of lucid intoxication that makes committing to something simultaneously unthinking and rational. I've written on the benefits of mindfulness as a methodological approach to heightened attentiveness in the world. After cultivating some mindfulness it's possible to experiment with a willful suspension of it. Mindless activity is often harmful and meaningless, but meta-mindlessness is spurred by, you guessed it, meta-mindfulness.

Meta-mindfulness is a self-imposed lack of overthought that allows us to just sit down and write, paint, eat, whatever. This is mindfulness in its truest and least forced form, enabling the trained practitioner to engage fully with the moment and do things without concern for what comes next. I didn't find myself developing this skill until fairly recently. We all fall into the common traps of misunderstanding when it comes to mindfulness and other spiritual works. We think it just means to focus hard and pay attention. But the mind can be focused while still overacting, overthinking and overanalyzing. We can be committed to false goals. The next step is to recognize which intentions are pure.

Meta-mindfulness is an aid to modern life. So many of our actions have endless layers of ulterior motives that we rarely stop to investigate. Mindfulness as a first step allows us to investigate our motives, develop self-honesty, and use critical thought to our advantage to peel away layers of falseness from ourselves. But meta-mindfulness allows for the further steps to be taken. Overthinking action is just another complicated form of egoism. The person who can't decide whether or not to act isn't more or less virtuous than anyone else; they just have a stronger ego-self conflict.

Indecisiveness and inaction are products of dishonesty with ourselves. The person who is always clear about their true desires and motivations is rarely hesitant about action. The term "intuition" comes to mind, but different people have varying degrees of intuition. Just because you exist doesn't mean your intuition is going to lead you down the mindful path. If your mind is cluttered with nonsense and falsehoods, which many minds are, your intuition won't help you much. But if you've found within yourself an ability to reach the essence of honesty, diligence, and self-discipline, you're likely to be able to access meta-mindfulness.

The best part about these post-mindful developments are that the mind becomes trained to initiate them when it needs to without much thought. It's why Samurai were trained to fight without thinking; they had cultivated enough discipline and mental clarity to do so through constant training and restraint. The muddled modern person uses conceptual thought as a crutch and is usually dishonest with themselves and others without even realizing it. Once this crutch is overcome, one can still live a mindful life without so much frivolous thought.

Solitude and Love

"Paradoxically, the ability to be alone is the condition for the ability to love." —Erich Fromm

The more I meditate, the more my idea of love evolves. I believe it has grown significantly healthier since my practice became more serious a few years ago. I've learned from numerous false assumptions about the idea of love and have tried to develop a more thoughtful and empathetic way of loving. I've also learned from lots of mistakes.

It's easy to see the world as 'out there', as something that is not you. The reality is different, though. You are intertwined with the world in millions of little ways. Most of these connections are unapparent. If we thought about them constantly we would go crazy. There's no need to think about them all the time. But recognizing the integral relationship between 'you' and 'the world' helps you shorten the distance between 'self' and 'other'. Over time, when you see yourself as part of the fabric of the world, you feel less alienated from others. Recognizing your faults as 'not your fault', you can make peace with them, love yourself, and subsequently love other people despite their 'faults'. Everyone's non-judgmental true self is beautiful;

just look at the wonderful innocence of children. Our perceived 'faults' come from subjective life experience and conditioning.

In recognizing myself as part of the fabric of the world, I become less narcissistic. My obsessive individualism fades. I am not necessarily a special snowflake, nor am I free to do whatever I want if I want to live a happy life. If I want to respect the wholeness of the universe, I must follow certain guidelines. In respecting these guidelines, like not harming others, I respect myself. But if I *only* respect myself, I neglect the guidelines at the expense of others, which ends up hurting me too.

This is why it is important to cultivate self-respect. When you respect yourself, you can be kind to yourself and others. You can love without need or expectation. This frees up a lot of energy that can then be spent loving yourself and others with more compassion.

When we attach too many selfish expectations to love, we become precisely what we fear. This doesn't mean we should let others step all over us or violate our basic principles. It just means we should not expect the world to conform to our every wish. Similarly, love is never perfect. If we expect perfection from ourselves or others, we will end every relationship in tears and fury. When we accept imperfection, love becomes accessible.

This way of thinking is refreshing to me because my generation is often selfish and ignorant about loving. Is this the result of their true nature? No, it is the result of decades of destructive and reductive cultural conditioning and life experience based on such conditioning. We learned from culture to be shallow, clingy, dramatic and selfish. Millennials are having less sex than any generation precisely because they are more hesitant to commit to selfless, devoted loving relationships. This is the supreme irony of narcissism: when you want to have your cake and eat it too, you are often denied both options. When you want it all, you get nothing. When we are too selfish about love, we spoil it for ourselves, precisely because real love becomes impossible when it is selfish. Love is the opposite of selfishness.

The key to a healthy idea of love is to be kind to yourself. Meditate and be honest with yourself about who you are. Once you know who you are, you can make peace with yourself and love yourself. When you love yourself, you can extend this love healthily to others who are in the same healthy state. Many people skip this step. They require love from others that they are incapable of giving themselves, and they create massive conflicts. The result is millions of people who don't know themselves pairing off with one another and feeling dissatisfied.

Finally, we should not be scared to avoid commitments and sacrifices just because they can hurt us. Getting hurt in love is one of the most important experiences a person can have. This doesn't mean we should try to set ourselves up for failure, but we also shouldn't postpone growth and change just out of fear of failure. The most important lessons I have learned in love have been through failure. As with most things, overcoming a neediness for love ends up allowing us access to it. The less you need, the more you have.

Sucking is OK

"Sucking at something is the first step."
—Jake the Dog

What sells? The quick fix. The rags to riches story. The pop star. The meteoric rise of the Hollywood star, the entrepreneur, the innovator, the Dionysian romance. These are the pervasive tropes of 20th/21st-century culture, and in America particularly, but *why* do we like them so much? Put simply, we enjoy seeing only end results because we are obsessed with results! Watching someone self-satisfied by simple activities isn't a very interesting entertainment experience.

The wonders of the upper-percentile of humans who have chosen to make themselves specialists has paralyzed the rest of us. Someone who's 25 and has spent 20,000 hours of their life coding, skiing or playing the saxophone could only be honest in acknowledging that there are other areas of their lives they have, either by sheer habit or necessity, neglected. Anyone who is accomplished in any field did, at one point, suck. Some of them *still* suck. What use is worrying about sucking? We only fantasize about results because we are terrified of committing to the grit of everyday life.

The goal here is not to instill in you a thirst for vapid accomplishments. I do not want to incite the herd mentality. The most interesting people in my life are not specialists, but eccentrics: the wildcards, the artists, the entrepreneurs. And these are people who have at some point decided that they were OK with sucking at a bunch of different things because they enjoyed action for action's sake. They sucked at being in love, they sucked at building credit, they sucked at guitar, they sucked at working, they sucked at investing. But over time, we overcome the tiny obstacles that make up our days, weeks, months, and years, and progress to something that doesn't suck. At that point it doesn't even matter, because we have learned to love the journey rather than the destination.

My intention here is to encourage you to do something you're bad at. If you don't feel like that, do the thing you're good at but focus on the areas where you need to improve. This practice helps us change the way we approach tasks. Instead of obsessing over the end results, we learn to find enjoyment in the process. It's the process that produces results, after all, and if you can teach yourself to focus on improving at every infinitesimal locus of each process, your work will take on a whole new meaning. Doesn't matter what the work itself is. Just do it with awareness.

Meditation helps us accomplish this. In focusing on the breath, we treat every tiny action as if it's a Big Deal. The little skills of daily life become the fruit of daily life itself. Like a Zen monk, we wash the dishes, make the bed, pour the tea, whatever. Apply this to your work, even if you think you're bad at what you're doing.

Culture gets us living in our own heads, constantly judging ourselves against people who've spent years paying their dues. The truth of the matter is that life is more about paying dues than reaping rewards. If we can make the due-paying fun and learn to find joy in the little actions and reactions of the day, we'll soon find ourselves not-sucking at the most important skill of all: life itself.

Those Who Know Don't Talk

The title of this post comes from one of Lao Tzu's most famous lines in the Tao Te Ching, a principal text of Taoist philosophy. The immediate reaction one might have is, "How ironic. Who's this guy talking at me telling me that those who know don't talk?" This only elucidates the simple brilliance of the statement. Lao Tzu is of course using language to remind us of the limitations of language— one of language's greatest gifts. Similarly, he is a master reminding us that he who considers himself a master is in actuality not a master at all. Only through doubt, skepticism and humility do we reach truth. Beneath the sly simplicity of Lao Tzu's writings exists eternal wisdom.

I find myself returning to the Tao Te Ching on a regular basis. If I could choose one book to give people who want to learn more about spiritual practice and Eastern philosophy, I would choose this particular book. Centuries before complex Western philosophical figures, this accessible text made use of basic language in an incredibly illuminating manner. Alongside its illuminations it reminds us of the fragile nature of the written word.

Back to where we started— how ironic that I of all people am writing an essay about not talking.

Having spent years reading and writing this sort of stuff, I have come to the conclusion that it's better to write about the fragility of language than to not write at all.

The primary purpose of this is that we should be conscious of not just what we say, but of how we say it. That doesn't mean fixating on being inoffensive and nice all the time; that behavior is growing in popularity despite being dishonesty and obfuscatory. More so, we should be conscious of *why we speak*. What's so important? I am an incredible garrulous person despite my mindfulness practice. Lately I've been trying to recognize when I'm just talking to talk. I find that this is often the case. Wisdom comes in silence, confusion in constant chatter.

It doesn't require much observation to acknowledge that the world has become obsessed with quantity over quality. Our speech, being an obvious reflection of the world-at-large, mirrors this tendency. William Burroughs said, "Silence is only frightening to people who are compulsively verbalizing." We have lost touch with silence.

There's an opportunity here— to exist in a world in which more information and linguistic richness is at our fingertips than ever before, but also to harness willful silence so as to make our words more thoughtful and impactful. Meditative practice is a special daily allotted period of silence in which the mind turns in on itself. Once the words fade away, truth begins to emerge. It's indescribable and can be frightening to a mind conditioned by the limits of language.

In Zen tradition, I'd like to 'kill the Buddha' that is Lao Tzu and revise his ancient saying. It's not that those who talk don't know and those who know don't talk. It's that talking often inhibits us from truly knowing. An inability to stop verbalizing alienates us from quietude, which makes it significantly more difficult to connect with the deeper metaphysical truths uncovered during silent reflection. The key is to practice more.

Don't Mind

"This is my secret, he said— I don't mind what happens." —Eckhart Tolle

"There is a Taoist story of an old farmer who had worked his crops for many years. One day his horse ran away. Upon hearing the news, his neighbors came to visit. "Such bad luck," they said sympathetically. "Maybe," the farmer replied.

The next morning the horse returned, bringing with it three other horses. "How wonderful," the neighbors exclaimed. "Maybe," replied the man.

The following day, his son tried to ride one of the untamed horses, was thrown, and broke his leg. The neighbors again came to offer their sympathy on his misfortune. "Maybe," answered the farmer.

The day after, military officials came to the village to draft young men into the army. Seeing that the son's leg was broken, they passed him by. The neighbors congratulated the farmer on how well things had turned out. "Maybe," said the farmer."

I've read varied versions of the idea that the purpose of Zen is to find the mind of no-mind or to go beyond thought. When we truly *don't mind*, what do we do? How does thought inform action? What do we think? What do we say? This is difficult to conceptualize since conceptualizing it negates it. Without mental faculty, we cease to 'be' in the way we are most comforted by. Modern society places such a high value on raw intellect, but at what cost? What are we trying to think so hard about? Does it really matter?

Intense thought must be balanced by intense non-thought. This is where meditation comes in. Meditation is a controlled exercise in un-minding the mind. When the mind is allowed to sit and reflect upon itself in silence, it eventually quiets down. Brief moments of lucidity emerge from the rubble like sprouts of trees emerging through the sidewalk. It's beautiful. The less we expect them and focus on them, the more they surprise us. This lucidity grows in strength over time and permeates everyday life in a way that enhances it without detaching it from reality.

The trap of attachment is that it convinces us that clinging to a million things is natural behavior. Attachment is natural in a sense, but most people attach themselves to things in an unhealthily intense way. They set unrealistic expectations in every realm of their lives and wonder why they feel perpetually dissatisfied.

When we constantly judge every tiny event against idealized standards of living, we lose complete perspective over the nuances and spontaneity of life. I find myself living more mindfully when I think about the story of the farmer. Events seem easy to judge in the moment but they often have future repercussions far beyond our capability of understanding. How often do we prevent the present from unfolding naturally by stubbornly trying to change uncomfortable circumstances? There's no use in getting too worked up about anything in the moment. Situations are only improved by keeping a level head and acknowledging that everything passes.

Programming Your Habit System

Human-as-machine analogies get shaky, but for the sake of all of this talk about "optimization" let's briefly forego all the weird dystopic sci-fi connotations and refer to ourselves as machines. What constitutes the human machine? What makes us function?

We've got hardware— physical bodies.

We've got software— psychological predispositions, subjective real experience, and subjective virtual experience (culture).

We've got accessories— what we own.

In this respect, we are more machine than we are special snowflake. People are "individuals" only to the degree that their collective subjective experiences and minor biological tweaks differ from others. Besides that, we're working with a unified mass of very similar machines. These machines get more similar as you group them based on religion, cultural ideology, ethnicity, nationality, etc. Even in the globalized world, people tend to group together based on these identifiers, so I cannot ignore their differences completely for the sake of a more simplistic argument. Another important thing to recognize is how tenaciously we cling to accessories that don't technically change our functioning that much. Most of us would be fine without ownership of much of what we hold dear— ideas and people included— and yet we bind to them as if they are the source of life.

So, we're a bunch of different groups of slightly-varied emotional machines going about our lives. Obstacles arise. Sometimes they arise as pure hardware problems (disease, severe mental illness, disability). Sometimes they arise as software problems (general suffering, acquired minor mental disturbance, addiction, bad habits). Usually our problems are a mix of complex interactions of these inner-facets of life with our external attachments. We worry about feeding ourselves and our families. We worry about death. We worry about acquiring or losing stuff. We worry about acquiring, losing or keeping people in our lives. We worry about the meaning of life. We get mood swings, fears, and uncertainties.

When problems arise, what do we do? Some people panic and let the problems slowly transform from surface-level disruptions into deep pathological issues that affect the actual composition of their software and hardware, like a virus. Most of us do this to some degree, since only an *actual* robot could ignore the emotional fragility of the human psyche. Things affect us, both internally and externally. Mindfulness helps us maintain a balance, though. When the internal world functions at a higher level, the external world becomes less important. When the external world is prioritized, the internal world suffers.

I use this long-winded analogy to try to elucidate the idea that habits are multi-faceted. A habit like smoking, for example, has endless implications. It has cultural implications. It has health implications, which in turn have financial and emotional implications, and so on. It has psychological implications; someone who forces stress upon themselves through a state of constant nicotine withdrawal is probably a generally *more* stressed-out person than someone who learns to naturally manage stress without nicotine as a reliably addictive middle-man. These implications all snowball into really important parts of our lives, and so it's important to reconfigure how we approach habits. Relationships with the external world that seem frivolous and simple can actually severely impact our internal lives.

I see this as the reason that people who "get healthy" sometimes get really intense about it. This happened with me recently when I decided to start eating a basic pre-modern diet of things like yogurt, eggs, vegetables, organic poultry, etc, basically my own version of the paleo diet. I started also lifting for an hour every day instead of three days a week. Lastly, I quit smoking after years of social dabbling. Smoking is a definitively modern habit that I think wonderfully exemplifies the absurdity of our post-industrial rationalizations for unnecessary things. Quitting was a symbolic act. It is unnecessary and merely complicates your mental attachments rather than simplifying them.

In the same way that trauma and tragedy sometimes set off changes in our habits that snowball into crazy new facets of life, the first few positive habit changes I made made me feel more at peace with being human. So I kept finding positive changes to make. These also made me feel better, which was incentive enough to stay consistent. Now I am eating healthier than ever, exercising more than ever, and not wasting time on bad habits.

This is a positive example of learning where problems arise and how complicated they really are, and tackling them with subtle changes in both software and hardware. Every day I fine-tune my hardware with exercise and meditation, which in turn fine-tunes my software in the form of less stress, better health, improved physical appearance, and higher self-confidence. These in turn make me feel generally better, which makes me work better, and so on and so forth.

Habits are the fabric of everyday life. Sometimes we start to let ourselves go and then feel like it's too late, since our software has been allowed to run with bugs for so long that it's forgotten what a state of normalcy feels like. People even convince themselves that normal everyday function is bad, that it's better to go against one's natural software and hardware. Is this a conflict that we are equipped to fight? Why start a war against oneself? We deny the fact that people are different and that part of this is by choice. The key here is not to treat ourselves like thoughtless robots, but to realize how much of life really is programmable to an extent once we recognize the relationship between theoretical software, hardware and accessories. If you aren't satisfied with where you are or how you feel, there are changes you can make to return to your natural self. And over time, these small habit changes snowball into larger parts of your life.

Pain is Fuel

"To those human beings who are of any concern to me I wish suffering, desolation, sickness, ill-treatment, indignities — I wish that they should not remain unfamiliar with profound self-contempt, the torture of self-mistrust, the wretchedness of the vanquished: I have no pity for them, because I wish them the only thing that can prove today whether one is worth anything or not — that one endures." —Friedrich Nietzsche

A lot of people are afraid to admit that life is just as much about suffering as it is about anything else. The more they deny their inevitable suffering, the more they suffer. Similarly, those who ignore their suffering, repress it or pretend not to feel it lose an opportunity to learn from it. Whenever we avoid reality it ends up catching up to us in more amplified ways. Pain is fuel to those who have their eyes open. Oddly, the more we plunge into pain and feel it fully, the more we are able to transcend it and work through it. Winston Churchill said, "If you're going through hell, keep going."

This is the paradox— people hate pain and avoid it out of fear, thus preventing themselves from learning how to properly deal with it. They create more problems and more pain simply because they aren't willing to deal with an initially unpleasant feeling. Think of how many addictions or violent actions have resulted from people who can't handle their pain from within and try to numb it. In cultivating mindful self-awareness, we save ourselves a lot of trouble. Pleasure rarely teaches us; it's not much work. That's why we gravitate towards it. We should respect discomfort as an opportunity.

This doesn't mean we should run around making each other hurt. There's enough pain in the world. The way of nature is inhuman and often quite painful. To be self-aware is to suffer. If you're alive and interacting with the world there's a certain amount of 'bad' stuff that's inevitably going to happen to you, the same way there are rainstorms and hurricanes. There aren't any places on Earth where these disasters occur in perpetuity forever. They occur periodically. Nature doesn't judge them; they're simply part of the grand machinery. The way of nature is to randomly apply chaos as a method of pointless change. Things are just always moving around and reconstituting themselves with no point other than to just keep going. The way to live harmoniously with the spontaneity of life is to follow suit. Just keep going.

This is making peace with the idea of entropy. Everything is changing; you are always changing. Whether you feel good or bad, you can't cling to the moment because as soon as you do, it's gone. Recognize yourself as a simple collection of natural particles subject to the same laws of entropy and decay as any other particles. You are subject to metaphorical erosion, difficulty, destruction, etc. From this reconstitution comes your evolution. This is the same phenomenon that causes people to be terrified of death despite its inevitability. In Zen mind, we meditate and make peace with all thoughts on every side of every spectrum. We let them come and go without grabbing onto any of them. Death becomes just another event in life. Suffering is the same. Why fight against something that we are completely unable to control?

Once we recognize all experience as part of the same life material, we stop trying to selectively curate our lives to be 'just right'. The more obsessively we try to engineer life to conform to our wishes, the more devastated we become when unforeseen problems arise. We can step back and relax a bit, recognizing that things are going to happen whether we will them or not. Similarly, we can learn not to take great experiences for granted, to understand that all we have could disappear at any moment. We might as well make peace with whatever comes along and work with it rather than resisting it or getting caught up in selectivity. Similarly, we should cultivate gratitude for life no matter what our present circumstances are.

Mindful Self-Control

"You can't calm the storm, so stop trying. What you can do is calm yourself. The storm will pass."
—Timber Hawkeye

Every impulse comes from a place beyond conscious thought. Most impulsive behaviors are spurred by deeper subconscious motivations. We are not aware of them. When they come about, we often act before we realize the extent of what we've done. This causes damage ranging from inconvenient to irrevocable, but in all cases it is unnecessary. Impulsiveness relies on mindlessness. It relies on the knee-jerk reaction, the sudden jolt, the emotional and unthinking response. It's usually detached from any sense of rationality or utility. It just happens. Many people resign to this. They think that they are who they are and that they *can* do whatever they want, that acting with impulsivity gives them total control. You *can* pour hot coffee all over yourself and let a taxi run over your foot, but that doesn't mean it's a good idea. Succumbing to indulgent impulses is really no different, it's just more abstract. The impacts are just more subtle. The cultivation of simple mindfulness counters this impulsivity and helps prevent unnecessarily harmful actions. It allows us to recognize what is unnecessary in life and to remove it.

Awareness of each breath in each moment brings about mindfulness. Mindfulness is a skill. It should be practiced and rehearsed in a controlled environment each day; this is the practice of meditation. When you rehearse full awareness of each moment in meditation, you carry this awareness into daily life. When you find yourself about to act on a poor impulse, mindfulness allows you to step back and return to the consistency of the breath and the present moment.

Stepping back further, you start to recognize just how much this curbing of impulse and increasing of mindfulness impacts your life. Think of how many subtle but strong ripples your poor impulsive decisions create over time. Laziness, vices, gossiping, neediness, oversleeping, overeating, giving up, getting angry, refusing to listen, refusing to understand, jealousy, fear, etc— these are all habits rooted in simple, small everyday actions. You are not who you are through and through; you are what you *do* repeatedly. These actions aren't who you are if you *shift* what you do. Shifting what you do helps you discover who you are because you realize that you are not actually trapped in long-established patterns of frivolous action and reaction. Training your mind to be consistently vigilant over these tiny actions is like inspecting each brick before using it to build a house.

Let the Dust Settle

*"Do you have the patience to wait
Till your mud settles and the water is clear?
Can you remain unmoving
Till the right action arises by itself?"*
— *Lao Tzu*

Sitting still is no small feat for the hyper-stimulated mind of the 21st-century. Nearly 40,000,000 Americans suffer from long-term sleep problems each year, with an additional 20,000,000 experiencing short-term problems— and those are only the people who end up seeing a doctor. Among these masses are millions more people who suffer from ADHD, OCD, depression, addiction and anxiety, among countless other debilitating conditions. Genetic predispositions aside, this phenomenon of modern history is obviously symptomatic of a larger problem: a widespread inability to quiet the mind.

Our distractions are inorganic. Science has developed not in congruence with nature but in *opposition* to it. We defy death and life with scientific and technological progress. This is an arrogance that has replaced religion in modern society— humans who feel dissatisfied as humans try to pretend they are gods. Abstractly thinking about this isn't particularly a huge part of the lives of most people, but the reverberations of inorganic life impact everyone. We have not learned how to exist in spiritual harmony with technological or scientific progress, and yet we continue to barrel forward at a resounding pace.

We spend more time in front of screens than we do in front of anything else. We cultivate multi-tasking and single-mindedness side-by-side. The average person's day is spent staring straight ahead at a self-imposed series of images for hours on end. Image becomes life and life becomes image. We lose ourselves in the black mirrors we stare at all day. I wonder if perhaps this has cultivated a simultaneous psychological inability to also look beyond the edges of ideological tunnel-vision. We are becoming less and less peripheral, less welcoming to ideas outside of a meticulously curated zone of comfort. We enjoy being able to thoroughly curate everything we experience and to cherry-pick worldviews. We're stuck in the matrix.

It only makes sense that this has led to a profound inability to cope with the unexpected. Our bodies are, after all, entropic masses of molecules no more or less immune to change than anything else in the natural world. Many things come up that we don't want to acknowledge. These experiences, not the artificially generated comfort images of our virtual lives, are the stuff of *real* life. They come and go and can really run us through the ringer, since we're less prepared to cope with discomfort than at any other time in human history. The reason we can't deal with the real is the same reason we feel stressed: we are distracted and looking 'out there' for salvation. The secret? True 'salvation' comes from looking within and seeing nothing is missing.

Meditation has resurged in opposition to this distraction. By looking within, we find spiritual depth. We equip ourselves with the awareness necessary to confront the unexpected discomforts of human life and be patient with them, contrary to the inhuman tools we've been provided with by science and technology. These tools don't help much; they usually just mask the problem. They teach us to avoid conflict and discomfort, to seek the path of instant gratification. And they teach us subconsciously to mask thoughts instead of confronting the bad stuff head-on. Meditation is the opposite of staring at the screen, enabling a starkly unspiritual (and dare I say anti-spiritual) generation access to an ancient practice of reflection and introspection.

This is of course what Lao Tzu means by letting the dust settle. Give the human mind a consistent degree of stillness and soul-searching and it will produce an organic morality of its own. This can differ slightly among different people, cultures, and areas, but a value system will emerge naturally from long-term meditative practice. Deep down, you know what to do. This is a real value system. It can cause people some discomfort initially, since it is often in stark contrast with the delusional proscriptive value systems we're fed by culture. There's no need for these isms if one takes the time to cultivate spiritual awareness. The dust of the conceptual world settles, and deep internal truths begin to emerge.

Long-term meditation practice will put you both above and against the plasticity of the modern world. We begin to see this imbalance when reading ancient spiritual texts. Read any of the ancient Daoist texts, or even somewhat recent Zen thinkers like Deshimaru or Sawaki. You will find not a guide to but an ideological medication for modernity. There is no striving, no vanity, no greed, no force—just a return to intuition, inwardness, and honesty.

Those who cultivate these values will find greatness in a world defined by its lack of such principles. Those who allow themselves to be dragged down by the external world of materiality will continue to feel enslaved, either consciously or unconsciously. Denying oneself easy satisfaction builds and deepens character. These concepts are not exactly things you'd see in a content-sponsored think piece or a TV ad. They have no profit motive. Sit attentively and let the dust settle.

Thoughts Aren't Real

There's a quote that's falsely attributed to Buddha—it sounds like a provocative statement but contains within it a bunch of falsehoods I'd like to address: *"We are what we think. All that we are arises with our thoughts. With our thoughts we make the world."*

In the realm of Zen specifically, these words are starkly different from the meditative mindset. But why? The belief that thoughts make the world is a comfortable idea. All you need to do to change yourself or the world is change your thoughts, right? If only life were so simple and solipsistic! Such a basic mindset is of course a lofty delusion but the world simply does not work this way. You can pretend the mirage is real but that's only going to detract from your quality of reality. Eating desert sand and thinking it's a sandwich won't prevent you from starving in the wilderness. While proper thought and 'right mind' contribute to a mindful life, thoughts also get in the way. Many of your most important decisions aren't made by consciously thinking but instead through deep spiritual intuition.

People seem to think that rationality comes from *thoughts*. The truth of the matter is that rationality and balance come from nature. Humans are natural creatures. Our processes mimic those of the world.

You wouldn't pretend to be able to time travel or teleport; these are contrary to what is allowed by nature, despite being fun humanistic fantasies. Why fight nature in the realm of day to day reality, then? Our self-aware thinking often clouds our intuitive organic rationality. The meditative mind cultivates this innate sense of balance. The more conditioning you are subject to, the further you get from reality.

The real lesson is that thoughts are rarely your friend. Conceptual understanding and 'knowledge' may point you to wisdom, but true understanding only comes when we transcend concepts altogether. These moments of awareness are beyond language. People of all eras and epochs have reported making crucial decisions during these periods of lucidity. The problem with most modern culture and human culture in general is that it trains us to be obsessed with thinking and analyzing. People think that they have complete control over who they are, what they think, and what they do. We pretend that we are behind the wheel of the ego. We have very little direct control, in fact. The thoughts that you hold most dear and are least willing to bring into question are often the most delusional thoughts of all. Those thoughts which please us most as fantasizing humans trying to deny our nature are often the *least* conducive to a meaningful reality.

Stop Looking

"To stop looking from any point of view is zazen."
—Kodo Sawaki

For years I have been trying to find a statement that adequately encapsulates what Zen has meant to me since I started haphazardly studying "it" as an 8th grader 10 years ago. This is difficult— all I've learned seems to point to the declaration that it is nothing at all, and that this is what is most important. That's its purpose. Meditation simply wipes your slate clean and enables you to embody beginner's mind. It is what allows you access to the whimsy and newness that makes children so insightful, but with a heightened degree of mature awareness. This is why it's so important not to meditate with any goal or purpose; to do so would be to counteract meditation's goal and purpose! The purpose is purposelessness.

An old master said something like, "Enlightenment is a matter of gold and dung. Before you get there, it's gold. After, it's dung." Similarly, I often think of the statement, "When you meet the Buddha in the road, kill him." What gets us to what the doctrine points to *is* the shedding away of the doctrine itself. Words help us by pointing us to the limits of words. This is the bizarre miracle of language.

Once we come to these types of realizations in meditation, we must cope with the fact that they're really nothing special. The profoundest experience is no different from the everyday experience. Such an understanding allows us to recognize everyday experience as profound. This way of thinking completely revolutionizes our lives when put into practice. Every tiny microcosmic action is an opportunity, not to apply a dogma or work on hashing out a point of view, but to live mindfully and humbly.

For this reason we can view meditation as existing outside of everyday life. We aim not to apply a particular worldview to our practice but to simply let all thoughts come and go. I mean all thoughts, not just the thoughts we like or don't like. Sometimes I'll be meditating and what I perceive to be a really incredible idea will float right into my purview. Instead of adhering to the Zen dogma and breathing through it, I'll stop briefly and write it down before getting back to sitting. Oddly, this keeps me less distracted. It allows me to leave the external thoughts in the external world. After doing this for years, I read Zen master Kodo Sawaki writing about how this is ok to do because it enables to mind to remain clear during sitting. Your intuition guides you towards right action.

Give your meditative self the gift of letting go of purpose over time. Don't meditate when you're stressed in order to become unstressed; you will get more stressed. Don't attach a purpose to this activity with a purposeless essence. Some people, especially Western practitioners, never realize what meditation is. They think it's a way to achieve their goals, to calm down and accomplish something. You may be able to accomplish things as a result of your practice, but it will be precisely because your practice will enable you to think neutrally and let go of the preconceptions and ambitions holding you back. In forgetting about our mental attachments, we free up lots of energy. This energy enables us to do more than we thought we could do before. But if we think about this during meditation, we miss the essence.

Expectation and Delusion

Expectation is a truly doubled-edged sword. People are often moved to action specifically by expectation and nothing else. Some sort of abstracted promise or reward can push people to take initiative in a way that they otherwise might not. Distant rewards inform even the most loosely-related actions. We want to badly to shape our lives around a single point, but this makes us unhappy and misdirected over time. Still, everyone develops a relationship to expectation. People who are driven and want to achieve this or that rely on persuading themselves to act through expectation.

Some of this is obviously cultural. Most of the things humans want to achieve, especially nowadays, are from a simple point of view entirely unnecessary. Buying a nicer stereo system when stereo systems used to not exist, buying a nicer house when you already have a nice house, trying to trade-up spouses as if they're baseball cards— people often act in this way. It's not uncommon. But it is supremely unnatural. There's no need to 'trade up' when you can sit and recognize that you already fundamentally have everything you need.

The answer to this conundrum seems reductive, but it does explain at least part of the problem. When we psychologically associate expectation and achievement, we make it impossible for the bar to reach any sort of ceiling. The ladder of potential satisfaction goes higher and higher and higher until the sun burns you. Modern life has made everyone into their own Icarus, flying so high that they overstep their bounds and come crashing back down to reality. The overdose metaphor always seems to apply to the basic tenets of desire, which is why drugs serve as such potent cultural and literary metaphors. We are addicted to little successes, to the point that we sometimes let them drive us toward ruin.

If a human being wants to achieve something, they set expectations. The desire in and of itself creates an extra layer of expectation— what they will feel and how life will be better after they achieve whatever it is they are trying to achieve. Self-conscious thought doesn't change the way the natural world works, and nature does not give a damn if you accomplish anything special. The fire in the library does not discriminate between good books and bad books. The tornado does not choose whose houses to knock down. Even if tomorrow you were to achieve your lifetime achievement, you would probably feel dissatisfied shortly thereafter. As the Zen saying goes, "Things are not as they seem, nor are they otherwise."

The way to moderate expectations is through doing things for their own sake. Instead of playing sports to become good at them, just shoot the ball. Instead of trying to become a master shredder, just play guitar. Mindfulness is the art of "just doing". The problem with expectation is that it adds a layer of unnecessary complication to doing, a layer that is potentially self-defeating. If you do a thing with an expectation, and it doesn't live up to your desire (as so often is the case) you experience fear, failure, detachment and laziness. Idol worship in popular culture makes us feel inferior, like we shouldn't do things unless we know we will be good at them. This is precisely what prevents people from getting good at anything.

The reason people are lazy is simultaneously the reason they are ambitious— they associate action with expectation. If they don't act, they don't expect, and thus they don't suffer. If they do act, they expect, and often do suffer. Projecting idealizations onto an uncaring and inhumane world doesn't make good things more likely to happen. It often just causes you trouble. The secret is to act without expectation, thus engaging the world without suffering for no reason.

Expectations are the simplest and most common of delusions. They are human beings betting present contentment on a future promise that, by nature, cannot ever be wholly fulfilled. This is the sad side-effect of what sets us apart from other species; self-consciousness makes us think we can project our desires onto nature and thus change nature's fundamental workings. We can't. Better to cultivate mindfulness, healthy detachment, and a lack of expectation, all while working diligently towards attempts at pure action and agency.

Understanding Karma

Karma is a peculiar concept. It has different meanings in different cultures, ranging from the accumulation of merit from past lives to the simple physical laws of cause and effect. Since we're not ancient mystics or monks, I'm going to err on the side of cause-and-effect. Contemplating karma can help us be more mindful of our thoughts and actions and the complex interrelation between things. It helps us remember that we are not independent agents in the world, but that everyone impacts us and we impact everyone in subtle little ways every day.

Understanding karma in this way contextualizes the idea in a way that changes how we approach living. Working on a definition of karma as something ordinary also makes it less intimidating. Who's to say if you had past lives? Who's to say if you will have future lives? Making weird proclamations like this is just as silly as trying to describe "God" or assign purpose to nature. As far as humans know, God has no appearance, nature no purpose. To try to create these things is beside the point.

When I hear the word karma, I picture a small pond. My life consists of my sitting by this pond with a bucket of stones of varying sizes. These stones represent the day-to-day decisions that make up life. There are stones thrown with vigor and stones left untouched. There are stones that make massive waves and ripple for hours and stones that ripple for a short while before the water returns to its placid state. The water always returns to this state; this can be compared to nature's indifference to human life. We are only important within a human framework of importance. We are no more or less valuable than an ant or a dog. If anything, the havoc humans tend to wreak out of sheer egoism puts them *below* the unselfconscious beasts they believe themselves to preside over.

Karma is simply the result of action. You do things. Other things happen. It's essentially how the mechanics of nature respond to your place within nature. What you decide to do is based on what you've done and what you want to do. Every action has a consequence, no matter what. No human is capable of perfectly understanding the potential consequences of every action. To try to do so would drive you insane. Knowing exactly what your actions will do is not necessary. Everything you do has some sort of effect on the world.

Combined with mindfulness practice and meditation, understanding karma in this way makes it less intimidating. For normal people, contemplating the potential repercussions of every little action can be a bit overwhelming. There's no need to think about this. The important thing is to focus on karma as a fresh seed rather than trying to hack away at the branches of trees you've already planted. Your actions come from a place deep within you. Everything you read, think, say and feel informs the way you act.

This is the most important thing to understand about karma. Every moment you spend reflects your karma. If you spend all of your time mindlessly worrying about petty problems, exploiting others and criticizing the world, you limit your spiritual development. If you instead devote yourself to learning, working, meditation, and mindful action, you set a more virtuous bar for your karma. Life today is not especially difficult. You can do very little and still survive. Many people do the bare minimum and rely on others to support them. This is not the way of Zen. Instead, we should aim to live simply, to work hard, and to spend our time as mindfully and compassionately as we are able. We should aim to transcend the ego and work past toxic thought patterns. All of this contributes to a more mindful life.

Working Life Away

When innovation began overhauling America in the first half of the 20th century, a bunch of economists started speculating about machines replacing humans as laborers. Some believed that machine labor would drive the length of the work week down while keeping income levels the same (or, ideally, raising them). Some believed that machine labor would lead to mass unemployment. Some believed that nothing would change; the mechanisms of the market are such that people would continue working the same amount and machine labor would simply enhance the opportunity for massive profits. A mix of these three outcomes weighing heavily towards the latter one is what has actually occurred.

The average workweek is still ~40 hours. In pre-Internet decades, the majority of non-executives left their work at the office. The psychological burden may have remained, but they were able to go home and literally not be able to do any more work until they were back at the office the next day. Today, plenty of people abstractly work far more than the amount they're technically supposed to. Technological advances in mobility mean that tons of non-labor jobs can *technically* be done from the comfort of one's home. Most people do not work from home, of course, but I know tons of low to mid-level employees that feel compelled to answer work emails and do busywork after-hours at home but still go to the office the next day. It's a strange dynamic.

I work for myself. I work hard and do a bunch of different things to secure my future in the best way I can, but I still have plenty of free time. Why? I'm not exceeding my labor requirements to make someone else a lot more money than I'm making. Being self-employed changes the entire perspective on work. The only person I can be exploited by is *myself*. I often take advantage of my labor mobility and work deep into the night, but I enjoy it because the work is mine.

Having more free time to live life has changed my approach to work. I work all day, but it's a mix of work work and life work, whereas my daily life as an alienated employee almost entirely consisted of work work. The day feels organic and symbiotic rather than rushed and compartmentalized. The point here is not to smugly proclaim, "Everyone should quit their jobs and become self-employed!" The point is that we've become brainwashed about work. When I worked for other people, my mind was not focused on mindfulness or even doing a good job. My mind was focused on getting the task at hand done, and usually taking slightly longer than necessary to avoid overwork. There's never too much grist for the mill.

That's where most modern workers' minds are, whether they're driving a snow plow or plugging away at an Excel spreadsheet. This mode of operation conditions our internal dialog to get home and say, "Time to do nothing. Thank God I'm done with work and can *finally* do *nothing*." And instead of this being leisurely, it often slowly impacts other external conditions that make us more unhappy and unhealthy, and thus worse at our jobs, and the cycle spirals until we're fat lazy illiterate underpaid schlubs. When I was following the conditioned script of work-to-finish, I didn't think about work as life. We pretend that the time we are working is not time lived, when we often spend more time working than living! This is nothing more than throwing our lives away. Life is work. When we hate work, we hate life and we don't do nearly as much to optimize conditions as when we enjoy work.

Once we reconfigure our attitude towards work, the time we spend working on ourselves and our loved ones ends up not feeling like how we've been conditioned to treat work. It becomes deeply personal and valuable work. And this is precisely the type of wonderful work we've become alienated to. Work towards what makes you feel alive, not away from it.

Zazen: a Flash Guide

Zazen is the backbone of Zen practice. Without it, you're only skimming the surface. Zen without meditation is talking the talk without walking the walk. Here's a simple guide to getting started.

1. Sit on a pillow or meditation cushion.

2. Sit in a position that keeps your back straight.

3. Hold your hands in your lap

4. It doesn't matter what you do with your eyes. Some people close them, some keep them open, some half-open. Just pick one and stick with it for your session. I like to keep my eyes closed.

5. Focus on the breath initially. Start by breathing through your mouth with a few deep breaths until your breathing is settled and consistent. Then breathe exclusively through your nose and keep your mouth closed.

6. Begin to count the breaths. In is ONE, out is TWO. In is THREE, out is FOUR. In is FIVE, out is SIX. In is SEVEN, out is EIGHT. In is NINE, out is TEN. Then go back to one. Eventually you won't need to count, but it helps keep your mind anchored at first.

7. Your mind will stray. Don't focus on any one thought and keep your focus on your breathing.

8. After a bit, just count each breath cycle. In/out ONE, in/out TWO, in/out THREE. Go to ten and then back to one. This is more challenging.

9. Push through the part of your brain that tells you to stop or to do something else or to dwell on a thought. Push through the belief that this activity needs to be productive or that it needs to feel good. These are the thoughts you are trying to transcend. Just keep your attention centered on the breath. Use the breath as your anchor.

10. Start by doing this 5 or 10 minutes a day, then gradually increase. I like to meditate for 20 minutes a day, no more, no less. You can choose whatever works for you.

Try to meditate without a goal and don't allow yourself to be swayed by distractions. The key is to patiently sit through thoughts rather than indulging in them and grasping. This will be difficult initially but gets significantly easier.

You're Always Alone

"If you continue zazen, your characteristics change. Your sad face is completely transformed, unconsciously, naturally and automatically. It's the Way that changes you, brings you back to a normal condition. You should not try to escape from loneliness by becoming too "diplomatic" or depending on other people. Solitude is good. Zen is solitude. Becoming intimate with yourself during zazen means being completely alone and also with the others, with the cosmos." — Taisen Deshimaru

Who are you when you meditate? You are yourself, sure, and all of your various levels of conditioning, but you are also silent, peaceful, and unmovable. You are returning to your true self. You sit solidly on the ground with your back erect and your mind tuned to the flow of the breath. Your breath is the rhythm of your life. It's involuntary. Instead of forcing it, you simply follow it. You let the breath come and go. With the breath comes life; with life comes thoughts. Let your thoughts come and go with the breath. Everything comes, but it never stays. It *always* goes. In Zen, we make peace with this. There's no use fighting life because it can't be beat. There's no hopelessness, stress, or clinging, because everything passes.

This is the state of peaceful solitude. In Zazen, you are entirely alone. There may be people around. There may be images of people in your head or specific names on your mind. These people come and go like the breath. You let them go. You welcome them in and welcome them out. You are entirely alone, always, even when you are with others. Why fight this undeniable truth? Why not let it liberate you instead?

When you cling to a thought, you lose the rhythm of the breath. You temporarily lose your awareness. In losing this awareness, you lose a certain sense of perspective and you deny life. You only cling to *thoughts* about external things; rarely are you holding onto another person with your hands. Rarely are you clutching money to your chest fearfully. You cling only to your *ideas of* these things. You yearn for what they represent and what they provide. Ironically, what they provide is generated within yourself. The happiness that other people "provide" you with is created not by them but by you. You have the control here. When you let this awareness sink in, thoughts become less powerful. In letting thoughts come and go with the breath, you let more of real life in. Over time, this practice of Zazen fills you with more and more life, more and more awareness.

Be Honest

At a certain point in my life I had to come to terms with the fact that I was being dishonest. I don't mean I was a liar or a cheat or a crook, but I was being dishonest in the way that all humans are, at some point or another, dishonest: I wasn't communicating properly.

Communication is deeply difficult to do properly for most humans because it affords us the ability to lie in tiny ways all day long. We lie to ourselves to a degree so that we don't even recognize that we are being inherently dishonest with others. We're careful about what we *don't* say. We always make sure to say what we think in the most innocuous way possible, so as to not produce confrontation. When presenting ourselves, we often adhere to an idealized version of ourselves that doesn't accurately represent how we really feel.

An aversion to confrontation just for the sake of being "nice" and "comfortable" is one of the most profoundly self-destructive things sheltered modern people do. We disrespect one another by not being more confrontational and honest. We merely perpetuate dishonesty by participating in it so passively. Not only does not communicating your true feelings hurt you and further repress you; it also hurts the person who has no idea what you're withholding. We all do this. We let problems fester because it's uncomfortable to bring them up.

My life changed in a profound way as soon as I decided to start really being honest with people. I'm not insulting for the sake of being insulting, but if I have a bone to pick with someone and it's reasonable and not delusional, I will pick it. The goal is always to get to better understanding. This starts, obviously, with being honest with yourself. Once you discover your real motivations and value system, you can have the confidence and understanding of nuance to present your dissatisfactions to another person in a productive way. They may resist them up-front, especially if you've been sitting on them for a while, but over time they will be grateful for your honesty. At the very worst, you will alienate someone but know deep down that you followed your sense of what is honest. Anyone who is not receptive to constructive honesty has work to do.

Once your internal thoughts, actions and words come into harmony, being honest with others becomes second nature. You may find there to be a rift between the life you've created in your head and the life that exists outside yourself. The key is to either make peace with this dissonance or let your capacity for mindful action lead you towards a more harmonious life. Sometimes we become honest with ourselves and find that we have people and things in our lives that are no longer mutually beneficial. It's OK to part with these. It's most important to be honest about why.

Being honest with yourself and others, from the proper vantage point, allows the people around you the opportunity to grow and change, too. Proper criticism is healthy in the same way that proper compliments are healthy. Improper criticism is just as harmful as improper compliments, because it is dishonest and manipulative. A thoughtful criticism offers someone the catalyst to be more honest with themselves.

If we all move towards a culture of honesty, where we don't obscure truth for the sake of comfort, we'll find ourselves initially more uncomfortable. We might even suffer. But we will rise out of that difficulty with a newfound strength, self-respect, and respect for others. There is no positive change without rupture, and sometimes internal conflict and external conflict are required if we want to get to the heart of reality.

The Art of Death

It's a known fact that humans are, statistically speaking, losing touch with our corporeal selves. Our bodies are collectively in a state of unmatched decay. To illustrate this in a simple fact that, quite frankly, makes me cringe every time I remember it, more than 35% of American adults are obese. That's 1/3 of grown adults who, either by circumstance or by choice, have neglected their bodies to the point that they become a public health burden. If cared-for bodies are the sign of a vibrant spirit on both a collective and intellectual level, one imagines a 35% obesity rate not signifying much hopeful news for us.

The purpose of this isn't to demonize fat people, but to elucidate a lack of spiritual priority in contemporary society. Science has developed as a means to practical ends: industry, healthcare, defense, space travel, etc. Science is not used to explore metaphysics; it is used to explain and optimize the *material* world. As soon as scientists start trying to explain things that they can't observe, they end up making entirely unsupportable theories even more ridiculous than those of astrologers, occultists, or practitioners of pre-modern 'traditional' sciences. As such, we live *longer* than other human societies before us, i.e. we've increased the general quantity of abundance, but the majority of people spend their time distracted from a grim reality.

Science, as the developmental force behind industry, has led us towards lives of plasticine artificiality. It seems counterintuitive to say, but this is precisely because science is anti-death . Death is impractical— it's bad for comfort, it's bad for business, and it's terrifying to the fragile psyche of the modern person who, unlike humans of past epochs, is unable to deal with even the slightest discomfort. An inability to be uncomfortable reflects an *aversion* towards death, whereas spiritually rich traditions almost always help practitioners work towards embracing death as an inevitability. Spiritual traditions view suffering as a catalyst for growth rather than something to be avoided at all costs. Instead of embracing death, suffering and discomfort as inevitable (and spiritually valuable) facets of human life, modern science and industry have attempted to negate them. This has thrust the unknowing masses into a state of terrified sedentary anti-spiritual stupor.

Meditation practice puts us in touch with death. Sitting in black silence is, of course, spiritually symbolic of the process of actually entering the unknown void we perceive as potentially existing afterlife. Meditation reminds us that, as autonomous esoteric creatures, we possess a mysterious metaphysical defense system that can be accessed at any time and does not require external software. This inner system is starkly antithetical to science; it is indescribable and unobservable. It puts us in touch with the spiritual forces of the universe; people of different cultures have named these forces differently over time, but every mystical tradition in both the East and West acknowledges this.

Through meditation, we get to meet death and shake hands. We're given the wonderful opportunity to look into the void and get comfortable with our inevitable fate. People who don't take the time to do this end up remaining terrified by death and in their fearful paralysis they take life for granted. This collectively leads to the spiritual and moral deterioration of large human populations, which is what we're seeing today. The further we move from forced survival, the more we need to cultivate mindfulness in order to make peace with ourselves. Engagement with virtuality and materiality far surpasses engagement with the inner-self today. As a result, people are unable to cope with themselves psychologically, spiritually and physically. What we misconstrue as the meaningless of life is really just an acknowledgement of how much spiritual reflection we have to do.

This is the real reason to meditate. Don't do it because it will make you more efficient at your job.

Don't do it because it will make you more patient with your kids. Don't do it because it will help you quit smoking or watch less TV or drink less whiskey. Meditation *will* help with all these things, but it will do so by helping you confront the supreme truth of death and decay, and thus make peace with the ensuing discomfort. Once we make peace with death, we can devote ourselves to the act of living. Everything becomes more beautiful— even a simple tree or flower is a masterpiece to the awakened mind. This is the aspect of the religious tradition and experience that we have forgotten. Once this shift in perspective takes place there's no need for narcosis or neurosis; one can simply be happy to be alive, and happy to know it will all end one day. That's what makes it so special.

Escaping Cultural Conditioning

"The nuclear and space age that we live in encourages the vigorous progress of science. But man has increasingly become obsessed with science and machines and lost touch with his essential humanity. Zen works to check this estrangement and restore intensity of awareness. If we know ourselves at all times, truth is where we stand, Rinzai said. Each morning Zuigan called: The Self! The Self! Yes, yes, he answered. He also said: Don't ever let others condition you."
— *Masunaga Reihō*

"Conditioning" is a term with countless applications. Today I want to spend a bit of time exploring what this idea of conditioning is in relation to mindfulness, where it comes from, and how it applies to Zen practice. The word 'condition' itself goes all the way back to the Latin *condicio,* which translates to 'agreement'. What is an agreement? It's a collective decision in which two or more parties come to some sort of concession for mutual benefit. An agreement exists, by nature, to benefit multiple sides at the expense of the total benefit of one side. The opposite of this is coercion, in which one side uses force to achieve what they want. An agreement or condition is a sort of stipulation by which multiple sides concede to *less* so they can all have *some*. We do this mentally when we settle on nuance rather than dualistic ways of thinking.

Now, let's zoom out a bit more and stop indulging in Political Science 101 . What is *cultural conditioning,* specifically? If we want to actually mindfully understand who we think we are, who we actually are, and why the dissonance between reality and concept causes so many social problems and anxiety, we have to, again, ask *what is this thing? What is cultural conditioning?* And, in this case, how does this relate to our sense of self? When we reflect on this, we stop denying ourselves the peace of true understanding.

Given the prior definitions of conditioning, agreement and stipulation, cultural conditioning is when a given society says to an individual: "If you have it your way, there's chaos. If I have it my way, there's absolutism. Let's meet somewhere in the middle." This is why people aren't allowed to act like beasts. It's why rules, manners and politeness exist. But it's also why many people today are confused. Why can't they have their cake and eat it too? Because in being born into a given community, you enter into an agreement in which you agree to behave in exchange for a certain degree of security and belonging. When you take the security part for granted, you start to pretend that you are a wholly subjective agent in a lawless realm. This happens wherever there are groups of humans. Every social situation or group dynamic represents a concession that, at least in theory, causes the least amount of conflict for each side.

This is where we run into trouble with culture. Culture affects how you deal with others, sure. 'Cultural conditioning' is a layer of behavior that you acquire against your primal nature as a man or woman of X or Y background in order to get along better in a given society with given ideals. This is what we all do. But this conditioning is more complicated than a simple interpersonal agreement because it affects your perception of *yourself*. Most people are not prone to reflection; they believe their conditioning, whatever it is, to be their identity. They cannot divorce the self from the spirit, or either of these from the ego. As always, where the ego rules, truth becomes a fiction.

Enter from stage left— meditation practice. Over time, your practice allows you to peel away the countless layers of confusing self-effacing cultural conditioning you've been carrying around for decades and simply exist as a being, without a body, without a mind. You can sit and *be*. This practice of reflection and mindfulness pushes you beyond the mere confines of humanity and all of your cultural conditioning. It allows you to communicate with a higher authority. Don't think of this as a God but more as the underlying depth and universal truth of existence. It does emerge eventually. It is peaceful and beautiful.

Over time, this obviously changes you. I walk around New York and wonder how many people identify with their clothes, their affects, their appearance, the books they read, the music they listen to, the company they keep. This is *all* cultural conditioning. How many decisions do people make with petty external motivations that they misconstrue as their own? Overcoming this vanity requires contacting your deeper self. In Zen this is referred to as the 'true self'. You want to move past the self you think you know and simply let the real self emerge. With this emergence comes strength. With this strength comes a desire to know reality as it is, to abandon ideologies, conditioning and concepts and to cultivate a sense of truth based on deep inborn intuition. This is the essence of mindfulness: becoming what you are.

Finally, self-realization helps cultivate the compassion that so many petty cultural ideologies on every quadrant of the political, social and psychological spectrums try to instill in their blind-leading-the-blind adherents. Instead of loving people conditionally, based on how disenfranchised, ideological, open-minded or appealing they are, you love them based on the recognition that you are all cut from the same cloth. *Everyone* has access to their true self. We're united by this inborn wisdom. We just feel so alienated from one another because each of us is wearing a different shallow mask of personality. We rarely reflect on this and as a result we feel distanced. Reconditioning requires making an *agreement with yourself*— you will trade some of your self-indulgent whims and ideologies for a certain amount of silence and peace each day. This adds harmony to your life and solves the problem of identity at its root rather than hacking away at the branches.

Cultivating the true self in such a way helps you see yourself for what you are and subsequently the world for what it is from the perspective of that self and beyond. Your actions harmonize with your thoughts. Your thoughts harmonize with your feelings. A greater balance is achieved. From this balance, a way of life that makes *natural* sense emerges. This is the source of real lasting happiness. It's a way of life with purposeless purposefulness rooted in simple action without fear. It is the essence of "just doing". Just sit. Just reflect. Just let it happen. Life has a way of guiding you towards balance.

Mindful Self-Discipline

Asking a distracted, indulgent modern person to exhibit long term patience is like asking a caveman to play a piano. We all talk about patience, but were trained to view it as something akin to waiting until after dinner for a cookie. Real patience is long term and is a statement of mindfulness and self-respect.

For me, patience has a few core sub-principles:

Consistency
Reflection
Outcome independence
Self-discipline

By consistency, I mean that the act of being patient requires constant mental and spiritual training. Forcing ourselves to meditate is one thing, but doing it every day as a natural extension of our life is another. Certain meditation techniques ask people to practice multiple times a day. This consistency cultivates real patience, because one who is lazy and indulgent will just say, "It can wait until tomorrow." That's the spiritual cancer of the modern times— self-aware procrastination. We say to the world, "My life is not worth living right now, so I'm going to put it off until tomorrow."

Reflection is the simple process of examining the self on a metaphysical level. In addition to looking in the mirror naked after working out at the gym, the patient soul goes a step further and looks into itself. Mindfulness means seeing through mere appearances. Sitting in quiet reflection enables a person to notice more subtle inconsistencies and imperfections in their inner-life, the same way we notice surface-level things like zits, fat deposits and ingrown hairs when we look into the mirror. Meditation also provides us with the strength and aforementioned consistency to tackle these problems not with fear or cowardice but with confrontation. They then shrink as problems.

Patience is also deeply rooted in outcome independence, or not caring about how things turn out. There are countless destructive cultural narratives telling people to be productive and "results driven" 24/7. Why? Well, in this case, results mean "the bottom line". The only reason Mr. Boss Man tells you to care so much about results is because caring about results makes him more money. In a business context, sure, this is understandable, but in life-at-large, caring about results turns us into nothing more than abstract shallow profit hounds. The Taoists taught us 2500 years ago that truly great achievements are made by those who focus on the task at hand rather than worrying about results. When we stop worrying so much about results, patience arises as an inner-strength that says, "I can wait this out." It returns us to a place of compliance with nature rather than defiance.

All of the virtues stemming from patience come down to self-discipline. We're surrounded by distractions that appeal to our lowest animal senses. Action films stimulate our fight-or-flight responses and sexual drives, as does pornography. Smart phones make communication a mostly thoughtless and instantly gratifying endeavor. Social media makes everything in your life the projection of an image or fantasy and then a statistic to be sold back to you as marketing data. Human beings are losing their sense of self-loyalty. Looking at base pleasures on a screen is more appealing to lowest-common-denominator consciousness than taking the time to look within. The difference is that looking within leads to long-term self-actualization and bliss, while looking at the screen merely leads to fleeting sensory pleasure that leaves you thirsty for more, more, more.

This all might sound severe, but it's really not. The key is to have some cultural and historical perspective on mankind's not-so-distant roots. Back when people were more concerned about actual survival, procrastination was less of an option. We're layered in so many cushions of comfort these days that we forget what it was like to actually have self-discipline. Even buying entertainment to support artists is an old school thing to do now. Stealing has become a popular value. We're not talking ancient Greece; modern tech is a relatively recent development. We have traded the working intelligence of the masses for sensational comforts and entertainments. Only a few people have true initiative and patience.

I hope that this will be some sort of fire under the collective ass to cultivate patience in ourselves. I am working on doing it myself. The key is to approach dissatisfaction over our modern malaise with a sense of initiative and mindful vigor rather than a feeling of hopelessness. Through spiritual reflection, healthy action, mindfulness and compassion, we can expand upon our knowledge and transcend our shortcomings.

You Have Nothing

"No man is crushed by misfortune unless he has first been deceived by prosperity." —Seneca

We all experience periods of profound happiness and excitement. This is the way of life. These are usually balanced out by periods of relative stagnation or even suffering; those experiences are part of life, too. Underlying both of these states is a peaceful core. This core is always present but we often forget it in favor of positive excitement or negative brooding.

We especially run into trouble when we credit ourselves for our own good fortune. It's important to work hard and do whatever you can to live fully each day, but when you begin to associate your ego with your accomplishments, you misconstrue your purpose in the world. We own nothing; anything we grab at is only ours temporarily. As such, we should be grateful for whatever we encounter and understand that we are not to thank for our own accomplishments. We are not as individualized as we think we are.

This is the difficulty of the ambitious mind— it always wants to grab the next thing, the greater achievement and bigger goal, and so it's never satisfied. Those who appear to be chasing satisfaction are often also further away from finding it than those who just sit around, precisely because they set the difficulty level for life at its maximum setting. Shooting fish in a barrel is easy; deep sea fishing requires patience and acumen— and luck. Stepping back and not obsessing over external motivations helps us put our fantasies in perspective.

If you are going to chase after goals and worldly satisfactions, do so with the understanding that you are who you are regardless of your standing in the world. Those who achieve great wealth, fame or acclaim often forget who they are with nothing and become unhappy. We have to remember who we are with nothing because that's who we really are. People wonder why they achieve their wildest dreams and find themselves miserable— it's because they forget their true self.

Meditation helps us access this true self. It's beyond the ego and beyond the material world. Getting to know it better helps us stay level-headed whether life 'out there' seems to be soaring or plummeting. Understanding the limits of the ego helps us know ourselves better and not overvalue times of prosperity. Such judgments hold us back. Those who identify themselves based on their possessions and achievements are committing a form of spiritual suicide in which they risk losing their sense of self should these temporary things suddenly disappear. It's why people go crazy when they lose their jobs or spouses. They forget who they are with nothing.

No matter who you are, envision yourself as a mere body. Tibetan monks often meditate on their own deaths and the decomposition of their own bodies as a way of reminding them that they're on Earth temporarily. Nothing we do or acquire can change the facts of life and death. When we make peace with this, we're ready to handle everything life throws at us, no matter what.

Remove Something Everyday

Nature teaches us the creative side of destruction. A volcano emerges and ravages everything in its path. Eventually, new land-forms emerge, harboring new life and reconfiguring the geographic patterns of the impacted space. I was going to list more of these metaphors but then realized that there are tons; I'll let you use your imagination. Nature is the best teacher. In contemplating nature, we learn the importance of balance. There is an old proverb, "Sunshine all the time makes a desert." Rain all the time swamps everything. And, most importantly, nature at large doesn't care what happens. Most environments that harbor life and its subjective beauty are subject to constant change and subsequent adaptation. Change is the way of nature. Everything that exists in this universe is subject to *some* form of decay. The destruction is what makes creation possible in the first place.

We humans come along and we're so naive and adorable — we think we can formulate these vastly false concepts of permanence and solidity. Whenever we think we've got it made, nature comes around to remind us that the world is not ours. We can invent ways to optimize it, but at the end of the day the world itself is not optimized to cater to our interests. If it were, we wouldn't learn anything. Everyone dies, accidents happen, stuff comes up.

That's the way it is.

A favorite poem by Stephen Crane:
"A man said to the universe:
'Sir, I exist!'
'However,' replied the universe,
'The fact has not created in me
A sense of obligation.'"

The unthinking and non-reflective response to our petty fears is a culturally popular form of nihilism. We see this in teenagers who are new to the indifference of the universe. It's a knee-jerk reaction to feeling hopeless and meaningless in a cold world. Over time, most angsty teens get over this. Nature happens to them in the same way it happens to everything and everyone else, and they are provided with more fodder for growth and understanding. We experience death and loss, love and attachment, success and failure. We *acquire* experiences in the form of memories, now more than ever, given the image-driven nature of culture. We get to know ourselves better.

The existentialist position of many modern folk is based on this same idea of experiential acquisition. It's important to get out there and *see the world, eat the foods, drink the drinks, meet the people, do the stuff!* There's a certain hopeless Epicureanism that permeates the culture of experience. Everything is a possible new adventure to be "photographed", both physically and mentally, and cached away for future reflection. But if we always want more and more, these experiences become nothing but fuel for the next thing. They won't satisfy you.

This is a natural human passion, a desire to soak up life and get the most out of it. It's commonly perceived as arising from a place of benevolence and enthusiasm, and it mostly is. But it's also led us to having a strangely arrogant relationship with nature. In perceiving ourselves as singular agents who exist to soak up life and acquire experiences, we start to recognize ourselves as the proprietors, ignoring the chaos and dynamism of the natural order in favor of a simpler humanism. We start to feel ownership over this world whose gifts we gobble up and whose time we so meticulously curate for ourselves, since we're given such a limited amount of it.

And so we reach Lao Tzu's acquisition stage. We build knowledge, gobbling up everything we can. We build a foundation. It's like a sculptor going out and buying the big slab of stone. If we stop there, all we have is a big rock. The next step is to start hacking away at the stone. This is what meditation and contemplation do. It's what real love does too. Once we've spent some time soaking up the source material and filling up on the world, we have to start chipping away, simplifying, and reflecting all the while. Of course this applies in a literal material sense as well. Most of us have too much stuff that we've acquired along the journey. In removing the unnecessary from our lives each day, we set a material precedent for the actual nitty gritty, which is a more esoteric thing.

The heart of this spiritual type of removal requires a certain degree of self-confrontation. You can stare lazily at a foggy mirror and not be able to see zits or boogers, but that doesn't mean they're not there. Meditation, over time, increases the accuracy and magnification of the mirror image so that we can accept it instead of thinking that the foggy image is the real one. We start off by seeing the self as we wish it was. Then we see the self as we think it is. Then we see that the self is not what we think it is at all. Then this false concept of the self starts to melt away like a wax mask, and a real face emerges.

A simple walk through the forest will remind one of this natural requisite of destruction and removal. We need the negative space to make use of the positive space, the rests to make use of the notes. The more dynamic and nuanced the relationship between growth and decay, the more severe and romantic life becomes. The choice of how to approach it is ours, but wisdom only forms on the basis of honest reflection generated in response to experience.

You're Supposed to Suffer

It's a weird type of human arrogance to think that people can offset the great universal balance of positive and negative. It's like trying to split an atom; we all know what happens when you do that. The more resistance we put up, the more reality knocks us back down. There are thousands of books out there trying to convince people that the secret to their happiness is nothing more than a bit of positive thinking. This is very much a materialistic reduction of the concept of happiness. Similarly, it teaches people to obsess over happiness— not such wonderful advice. You know the least likely way to find satisfaction? Chasing it.

The search for satisfaction itself is *still* beside the point. Is life really just a big meal in which we eat until we're full and then we go to sleep? I don't think so. The more I've suffered in my life and also understood the sufferings of others, the more I've noticed a pattern. Those who are mindful and contented tend to take their sufferings in stride, as if they have no other choice. When they suffer, they suffer fully— they feel the feelings, cry, fight and do whatever they have to do not to hide their suffering, but to move beyond it. We're *supposed* to suffer. It is the condition of consciousness, our blessing and curse. Modern living has made us think that suffering a burden to be surpassed, but surpassing suffering merely means dulling our consciousness. Suffering will never go away, not without severe consequence. We either learn to take it in stride or we miss out on an important part of living.

Many people have a narcotic attitude towards suffering. It terrifies them and makes them uncomfortable and so instead of building a tool set for overcoming it, they aim to stifle it. The sheer popularity of entertainment, junk food, porn, video games and all these other modern distractions is testament to this. People have been led to believe that life is about satisfying pleasant impulses rather than experiencing all emotional states fully. They might not even be conscious of it; these distractions are provided to us as entertainment but they all serve as narcotics. The rise of tech and the rise of opioid abuse parallel one another. No surprises there. We've forgotten how to suffer.

I like to think that the concept of justice emerged as a reflection of nature rather than any sort of forced humanistic rearranging of the world. Justice is simply a human way of mediating cause and effect. For every action, there is an equal and opposite reaction. If you kill someone, something different is going to happen to you than if you eat a piece of cake. Just like humans, not all offenses are created equal. The scale of justice is reflective of a real natural process, and the entire concept of justice is merely a metaphor for something we've learned from nature— *cause and effect*. We don't give the murderer a cake just because that would create more temporary happiness in the world. No one is spared suffering no matter how 'good' they are, because nature doesn't care.

The scale of circumstance is not "happiness" and "unhappiness". There are a lot of "happy" people in this world and a lot of "unhappy" people, but this doesn't matter. Chasing happiness rearranges your life so that you prevent yourself from taking the risks and enduring the suffering that's likely to provide you with any sort of lasting awareness or wisdom. And that wisdom will always be offset by more suffering, so it's important to learn to navigate the world in a way that isn't just centered around constant happiness and well-being.

I enjoy certain Buddhist concepts to an extent but I don't value asceticism at all. Zen Buddhism is the self-critical form of Buddhism; it does not aim to get rid of suffering but to cultivate its conversion into wisdom, to sit through everything— good and bad— until we cease our petty value judgments. The four noble truths of capital-B Buddhism function using a definitively life-denying logic, and for this reason I'm truly skeptical of them. The essence of Buddhism is to challenge ideology, so let's challenge Buddhism:

Life is suffering
Suffering comes from attachment
Ending attachment ends suffering
Practicing the Noble Eightfold Path ends suffering

In a strange way this is just an esoteric ancient example of the exoteric modern self-help book mentality; it makes sense that such a mentality drew heavily from the Westernization of Buddhism. One can suffer, recognize one's attachments, and seek to end this suffering through various forms of ascetic goodness, lovingkindness, and whatever else, sure. This is cloaked in this religious concept of samsara, whereby one escapes being birthed in the natural world of suffering until one escapes the cycle. It's one way to approach life. Asceticism is by nature somewhat life-denying, however. As with anything, you're trading something else for it.

This is real life; there is no escape. If you want to play, you've gotta pay. If you do decide to escape, real life (nature) will respond by punishing you, as it punishes every action with an equal and opposite reaction. Those who balk from life may escape it, but those who escape also miss out. The more we take suffering in stride, the more we learn and, most importantly, the more we become immune to the disgruntling issues of the day-to-day. I want to suffer and learn from it and then suffer some more and learn from that.

Mindful Relationships

"As an ancient said, if people today were as eager for enlightenment as they are to embrace their lovers, then no matter how busy their professional lives might be and no matter how luxurious their dwellings may be, they would not fail to attain continuous concentration leading to appearance of the Great Wonder." —Man-an

Spiritual texts often emphasize the importance of solitude. To be properly alone is to cultivate a meaningful relationship with yourself. Unlike relationships with others, the relationship with the self requires honesty if you want it to progress *at all*. People can often get by without making meaningful connections to others. Many social adult relationships are just about sharing resources, networking, or feeling less alone. When it comes to the self, though, all meaningful relationships with others depend on your ability to be comfortably and mindfully alone. The meditative mind recognizes when it is clinging to others or using them to feel less alone. It works to detach from these unrealistic expectations of others and to develop peace from within.

The best relationships with other people are by nature *unnecessary*. That is, they don't come from a place of falseness or neediness; they just naturally emerge. True friends don't require anything of one another; each party can enjoy the company of the other without needing anything, wanting anything, or having to force any sort of interaction. Anything that is forced is dishonest. Trying too hard represents a lack of self-satisfaction. It emanates from people who do it and makes them less appealing to others. Having expectations of others is like demanding interest on a loan no one ever asked for.

Expecting too much from people stems from an unexamined relationship with the self. The narcissistic impulse to seek constant positive affirmation from people represents a lack of affirmation from the self to the self. When we do not accept ourselves, we try to force other people to give us more attention. If you truly love yourself with peaceful strength, you will require less of others, and your relationships will improve. How many potentially great relationships have been squandered by needy people who thirst for sex, money, attention or affirmation?

I love the prior quote from Man-an because it elucidates how people look outside of themselves for satisfaction. Those who look within and cultivate spiritual life through meditation practice find satisfaction. They build the courage to face the world alone. In developing this skill, they become better 'people people' than those who rely on others for their fulfillment. Humans are spiritually self-sufficient creatures if they choose to be. We require nothing in the external world to cultivate the life of the spirit. In fact, the more distractions and diversions 'out there', the more difficult people find it to look within. That makes meditation all the more special today in an era rife with distractions and vanity.

The key is to shift our priorities. Meditation helps with this. Think of how many movies you've watched in which people exhibit co-dependence and how many song lyrics you've subconsciously memorized in which people "can't live without" each other or "will die without" each other. The same way people think they need money or need fame, they think they need one another. Relationships with others can be a wonderfully rewarding and beautiful facet of life, but they should not be its focus. The focus should be your relationship with yourself. Once that's healthy and your ego is manageable, you can bring your best self to interpersonal relationships. What is selfish is expecting others to fill your void for you. Why not make peace with the void? Meditation is an invaluable practice because it hacks away at the roots of our unnecessary attachments and neuroses. The solution to many problems is the cultivation of mindfulness and detachment from expectations.

How to Relax

You're born into this world an empty slate, and it's not long before you're taught how to be stressed out. Everywhere we look we're exposed to environmental stressors and unnecessary worries. We're often certain that we need to buy stuff to be happy, or that we're stressed because we need to just work harder, or follow a certain authority, or whatever. The truth is that the key to relaxation and finding inner peace doesn't rely much on work, culture, or consumption. This should be a huge relief, since regardless of where you live, what you believe, or who you are, your stress is probably the result of one of the below factors. Take small steps to eliminate these factors, or at least minimize them, and you'll find more peace and relaxation.

A reminder before we start: *the world does stuff to you, but your life is determined by how you react to it.* The power is in your hands. Don't try to convince yourself that you're helpless, or that things can't change. Change is the essence of everything. Embrace it and catalyze it if you are feeling helpless or dissatisfied. We often prevent change by clinging to old ways of doing things that harm us.

Factor One: You care too much about results.
If Caravaggio had just stood in front of a blank canvas in nervous anticipation, unable to imagine how the hell he could possibly transform it into a masterpiece, he would have never painted anything. If James Joyce hadn't just started writing, he would have had a hard time writing Ulysses. The problem with modern people is we care too much for instant pleasure. We love our phones and laptops because they give us little bursts of dopamine whenever we accomplish the most simple of tasks. But give a modern human a blank canvas, a huge project, a relationship, or a new skill to learn, and they'll probably get insanely overwhelmed. The tasks that make life feel meaningful are those that teach us to immerse ourselves in the present moment.

A lot of our day-to-day functional stress comes from thinking too much about results. If we mindfully participate in the *process* of getting stuff done, stuff gets done. You do big things by doing lots and lots of little things. There is no other way.

Factor Two: You care about how you come across.
The problem with being raised watching images of beautiful people interacting and living idealized written lives on screens is that most of our reference points for life are just that: references. Instead of memories from real experiences, we

often rely on falsified made-up fairy tales, aesthetically engineered fictions, and outright false assumptions in our daily navigating of the world. Our collective obsession with images has led us to trust too much in mere appearances. For some perspective, let's look at a few figures:

Publishing generated $28 billion in 2015— that's every magazine, book, subscription, etc sold in total. Cosmetics, on the other hand, generated $60 billion. Plastic surgery generated another $14 billion. This is just one example to elucidate the point that modern people care far more about appearances than actual substance. This is obviously cultural and hasn't always existed as a predominant trait in humans. As individuals, we can reverse this obsession with surface level appearances and work on improving ourselves from the ground up, not by changing how we look or feel, but by discovering who we actually are. Meditation has helped me care less about how I come across to others. Instead of putting on airs, being a poser, or being pretentious, I have found a way to behave naturally. With mindfulness, we don't care about how we come across.

Think about how much time, money, and stress you can save when you stop worrying so much about keeping up appearances. The world rewards you for it. Since I started meditating seriously and caring less about petty material things, I've had more 'success' than I could have imagined when I was obsessing over my own perceived value. Mindfulness frees your mind enough to help you actually live a wholesome and fulfilling life.

Factor Three: You're not being honest.
We've all lied to others. It happens, unfortunately. Think about how lies work— they usually start small. Then, in order to bolster the initial lie, you have to keep lying. Pretty soon you're entangled in a whole web of lies, and you have no choice but to give it up or risk total annihilation. This is no way to live! Lying to ourselves works in the exact same way, but we do it far more often. The opportunities to lie to yourself are far more prevalent. Meditation helps us learn to be completely honest with ourselves at all times. This is a hugely important skill to learn. It can be painful at first, since most of us have built up giant snowballs of lies that we elaborate on to shelter ourselves from the reality of the world.

The best way to uncover these lies is to ask:

What do I really want out of life?
Who is most important to me?
Why do I do the things I do?
Am I honest with other people?

Telling the truth in daily life will completely change your life. People become unhappy over time because they lie to everyone— they pretend to be nice and let the world bat them around until they don't know how they ended up a complacent, helpless doormat! Be honest with yourself and others. If someone is being an asshole, talk to them about it. Don't pretend. Don't posture. Don't be nice as a false front. Better to be "mean" and honest and reconfigure your life around your actual intuitive preferences than to just be falsely non-confrontational with everyone all the time.

Varieties of Anxiety

I once upset a bunch of readers for saying that anxiety can be cured through mindfulness and meditation. Most responses were from thoughtful users who understood the nuances of the statement. But a few people were revolted. "This is bullshit." "This is the dumbest thing you've said yet." "Anxiety is a chemical imbalance." Whenever I strike a nerve, I know that there is an important lesson to try to understand.

I'm not a psychiatrist, but my grandfather, Sandy, was an early psychoanalyst. He came up at a time where Americans were just learning how deal with these new conditions. Anxiety was not a popular concern. Depression was not a popular concern. Homosexuality was still considered a mental illness. There was both confusion and naïveté in the field. It is still recovering from its attempt to objectively sort human behaviors into objective definitions of "normalcy". The human mind is vastly more complicated than we think, and the best way to navigate it is to reflect rather than trying to find external 'cures'.

Fast forward to 2016. Homosexuality is thankfully no longer a medicated mental illness! But new ridiculous habits in the field of psychiatry have emerged. "Anxiety" "depression" "schizoid" and "borderline", all legitimate diagnoses for severe conditions that, in those who suffer from them in a debilitating way, are actually life-threatening and chemical, also appear in smaller amounts in all of us. They're buzzwords now. Regular humans are often, by psychiatric standards, thought to be severely ill even if they can function perfectly well in society. It's like when you go on WebMD with a common cold and leave thinking you have esophageal cancer. Back to the point. We are human beings. We all suffer. We all have our demons. If we didn't we would be remarkably uninteresting. We wouldn't innovate. We couldn't create art. We wouldn't help one another with the same sense of compassion and empathy. Thank god for our small quirks, neuroses and sufferings! They teach us wonderful lessons.

I apologize to the suffering people who I may have offended by saying that through mindfulness and meditative practices we can cure anxiety. For those with severe chemical anxiety, this may not be immediately possible. But, statistically speaking, the vast majority of humans are *not* severely mentally ill. If they were, we'd have to shift the scale of sanity and normalcy to compensate for our collective insanity!

The truth of the matter is that most of us do suffer anxiety unnecessarily. We are living in very strange and chaotic times. Our attention is being bid for at all hours of the day by abstract forces who want to sell us stuff. The intimate details of our lives are collected for profit. We're able to communicate with anyone anywhere at the push of a button. And yes, it does drive us all a bit insane, seeing as it's a supremely inorganic privilege. We drive this artificial anxiety away by returning to our primal nature. We exercise. We eat wholesome foods. We sit in meditation everyday. We practice compassion, mindfulness, discipline and self-respect in our daily lives.

The problem with psychiatry is that, for the sake of profit and bureaucratic nonsense, a large number of completely well-adjusted people have been convinced that they need to be fixed from the outside. This is often simply not the case. I know numerous people who have been rendered helpless pharmaceutical addicts thanks to poor psychiatry. They've been able to recover their lives through practices like meditation, exercise and hard work. Our demons exist for a reason. Yes, sometimes they're caused by severe imbalances and require brain medicine— a modern luxury, with all the nuances and pitfalls included in the small print disclaimers accompanying most modern luxuries. Most of the time, however, we suffer as a learning opportunity. We have obstacles to push past, chaos to breathe through. We suffer from poor body image so we can learn to exercise and respect our bodies. We suffer from bad relationships so we can exterminate the lies and egoism in ourselves. We suffer from terrible jobs so we can eventually have the courage and honesty to find something valuable to do.

If we convince ourselves that our problems can't be fixed, that we can't work to improve ourselves, why not just hole up in fantasy land with a bunch of drugs? Most of us are blessed with the power to live through and work past struggle. We should *not* take this blessing for granted. Without challenges to overcome, life becomes nothing more than a boring zero-sum game. I hope that you can find ways to sublimate your anxiety and sadness into value for yourself and others. Create art. Learn new skills. Read great books. See nature in yourself and yourself in nature.

The Cult of Happiness

The cult of happiness is making us miserable. The happiness that obsesses popular culture is but a brief pleasure reward for desired events and behaviors, like a treat for a little dog. Somehow the gently feeble minds of the masses have been convinced by self-help culture and the tech mentality that human happiness is a mountain peak that we will all colonize once we figure out how to stay up there for more than a few minutes without falling off. This couldn't be further from the case. Happiness is a climax, meaning it's dynamic. It relies on the buildup of prior events, which requisitely must *not* be the same events that lead to the burst of happy feeling. The uncertainty about the health of one's newborn baby leads to the period of relieved happiness when it's found that everything is ok. The staying up wondering if the person you had a date with is going to call you back is a period of uncertainty that strengthens the eventual release— *should it occur*.

This *should it occur* is tantamount to the popular concept of happiness. It resembles a dramatic plot, which most people have been subconsciously programmed to project as a framework onto real life. If this conception of happiness is a gamble, which it is, then we're all problem gamblers. We stake the opportunity for present contentment on a potential future reward. The longer we wait and suffer for that potential reward, the sweeter the little dope burst feels if and when it finally hits. Perhaps "happiness junkies" is more sufficient term? If you've ever known a junkie, you'll know precisely *why* addiction of any sort is a dead end. When we become too obsessed with happiness, we give up on life. We trade the infinitude of now for a delayed *perceived gratification* later. We become unable to deal with suffering rather than learning from it.

Uncertainty only adds to the jackpot. But, like a junkie, the hits don't hit as hard over time. We experience a few humble successes and begin thirsting for more and more. We may even surpass our wildest expectations in accomplishments, but the receptors have weakened from years of abuse, and it's never enough. This is where the mass cult of happiness leads us, towards blind mindless dopamine addiction.

What to do? Overcoming this trap is not as difficult as it seems. It mostly requires an initial realization, a breaking point. You might wonder why so many famous and successful people eventually find spirituality— it's because they found themselves with everything they'd ever dreamed of but realized it would never be enough. The material realm is not the realm in which human beings become self-actualized. There's no house big enough for your soul's aspirations. No matter what you have in the fleeting external world of possessions, your mindfulness will be what delivers you from thirst and desire.

This is a beautiful thing; it means that your position in the world does not matter. Whether you're a bum or a CEO, you have a choice: direct your attention outwards or inwards. Focus on chasing the elusive carrot stick, or focus on your innermost truth. Meditate, meditate, meditate. As we cultivate inner-truth over time, it doesn't matter what happens outside. Instead of obsessing over little hits of happiness, we make peace with the inevitable suffering that precedes it. We might even try willfully subjecting ourselves to suffering as a test of inner-strength. Popular culture does not give the spiritual element enough credit; it makes it seem like just another way to acquire stuff and feel good about yourself. What it actually does is cultivate a resistance to weakness, mediocrity, ignorance, and vanity. Transcendence means, of course, *rising above*.

Say Thank You

"If the only prayer you ever say in your entire life is thank you, it will be enough." — Meister Eckhart

Perhaps there's some sort of parallel between attempting to be an entrepreneur and having a God complex; I didn't start reading religious texts outside of the Zen tradition until I became my own boss. Mysticism is a way of approaching the world rather than any sort of religious dogma. The word God refers not to a magical man in the sky who listens to us when we pray for a flat screen TV; God is everything. Aristotle broke God down into little units, Leibniz broke 'him' down into Monads, modernity broke 'him' down into metrics for efficiency and profit.

Most science breaks God down just enough to be able to reform 'him' into a cohesive logical superstructure that enables humans to make material advances. Spiritual advances are, of course, left on the back burner. Even the discovery by science that meditation influences brain chemistry does nothing but confuse people into meditating for the wrong reasons. If God is an all-encompassing term not just for what we see in nature but also for what we don't see, can't see, or won't see, proper prayer can be seen as a return to nature. Prayer is not greed; it's gratitude. If you're asking for stuff on a selfish whim, you're doing it wrong. In thanking nature for whatever we're given, we give ourselves the courage to jump back into the current rather than trying to assert a fragile human idealism onto nature. Nature doesn't care; this is what ensures its dominance. Humans are self-interested creatures; nature is not a creature but instead encompasses all things. It knows no such thing as subjectivity. And our subjectivity is almost always what leads us astray.

In saying thank you, we give ourselves some time each day to exit the world of human subjectivity. In the realm of staunch individualism that's run rampant over the past few hundred years, nothing is ever enough. Science stops for no one. Technology will continue to evolve as people continue to buy more and more stuff to satiate themselves. The more we desire, the more problems we create. The more problems we create, the more problems we solve. This is the false appearance of progress. Our progress isn't the result of growth; it's the result of unnecessarily solving unnecessary problems. It signifies our growing collective inability to cope with nature, to exist alongside it in peace rather than constant egoistic conflict.

In identifying with nature rather than this false narcissistic rift in human consciousness (a rather recent development in our history), we find a new contentment. Spirituality and materialism have never been fully compatible. We can exist in this materialistic human world, but once we begin to reflect we recognize its limitations. By its very nature materialism is incapable of providing us with what we're looking for. It is designed to fulfill invented necessities. Everyone loves to say, "Necessity is the mother of invention," but we never stop to question what we actually need. Humans of yesteryear would be shocked by our present-day technological situation. Are we any more spiritually sound? Happier? Engaged with ourselves and the world? No. We're more commercialized, self-gratifying and ignorant than ever. I'd rather think the world to be flat than think it revolves around me.

Stop Comparing

Living a life of mindfulness and gratitude requires people to stop comparing themselves to one another. The problem with these comparisons is that they assume some sort of overlap of life experience. It is difficult to truly embody the perspective of another person. Each life is so extraordinarily different, even among the closest friends and family members. People share many motivations and experiences, but that doesn't make it any easier to accurately understand the complex motivations of another person. To pity is to patronize. To idolize is to dehumanize.

You truly do dehumanize whoever you compare yourself to. Idolatry functions in the same way. When people idolize celebrities, wealthy individuals or 'successful' people, they remove them from their humanity. They place them simply within a realm of subjective idealism and wish fulfillment. People subject one another to constant ridicule, jealousy and bitterness based on false ideas of entitlement when they can never truly know what goes on inside the head of 'the other'. This is why all ideologies that choose a common enemy become dangerously dehumanizing.

Simple example: you believe your happiness to be caused by a lack of resources. You look at a wealthy person lounging by the sea with a cocktail and think, "If only that were me. I would be so happy." But can you truly enter the head of that person? Do you know that they enjoy lounging there any more than you enjoy lounging wherever you lounge? Does that temporary enjoyment even have any meaning? You can't know. If there's one true fact about humans, it's that we're born to adapt. If you aren't happy poor, you won't be any better off rich. If you can't be contented alone, you won't feel contented with your soulmate. Get the idea? The power lies within you, not in the outside world. Spiritual living is the great leveler. It is accessible to anyone who is willing to work at it. It doesn't matter who you are or what you have. The strength you need is within yourself.

The most important point is that when you compare yourself to others, you dehumanize *yourself*. You mistake your interpretation of others, but on top of that believe that judging yourself against this inaccurate interpretation is a good idea. Both are falsehoods. The way towards mindfulness is to acknowledge yourself as you are and to act as diligently as you can each day. Mindless comparisons and "have nots" only perpetuate the cycle of delusional attachment to external things and ideals.

All notions of paradise are dangerous because they presuppose that paradise can never be right here, right now. It's always somewhere else. The fact of the matter is that right here and right now are all we have.

Make Peace With Yourself

"Letting go gives us freedom, and freedom is the only condition for happiness. If, in our heart, we still cling to anything — anger, anxiety, or possessions — we cannot be free." — Thich Nhat Hanh

There's a lot of lofty talk these days about people with strongly differing realities making amends with one another. Idealists try so hard to convince mindless people to simply be mindful and love one another. That's cute and all, but mindlessness is defined by a lack of perspective and an inability to listen. Question any of these idealists and you will see precisely what I mean! You often can't get a message through to a mindless person because it's incompatible with their cultural or spiritual programming, regardless of what they believe.

When you cling to ideals, you create a false dualistic vision of the world in your head. You see good and bad in opposition, and always somehow see your position as 'good', unable to acknowledge that, to someone with different programming, you are the enemy. Such is the trap of dualistic 1 vs. 1 thinking. It's egocentric. It causes you to create enemies on the flip-side of your own righteousness, which provides you with a shallow but convincing sense of meaning. You then become immune to criticism— a fatal flaw. When you stop listening to feedback, you become bugged.

Instead of trying to force people to get along with one another, we should instead implore them to reflect on themselves and to learn discipline. The only people who are capable of getting along peacefully with others are those who have made peace *internally*. This requires strength and commitment and it's why most people remain mindless, idealistic and lost in delusion— they aren't willing to put the work in.

With steady meditation practice, we move away from the ego and toward the true self. We cultivate inner-peace. Instead of mistaking zeal and stubbornness for true strength, we recognize that strength comes from intelligent malleability, not violent rigidity. Only the person who can grow spiritually and psychologically will find peace in a rapidly changing world. When we cling to ideas, we buy into the chaos and begin to identify with it. We move away from reality. But when we make peace with letting thoughts come and go, and letting ourselves evolve, we can reflect with awareness.

Do A Thing

The American painter Jasper Johns wrote a note in his sketchbook once. It read:

"Take an object / Do something to it / Do something else to it. [Repeat.]"

I'm going to preface this by saying that the previous statement is an obviously simple approach to creating art. As such, it became the credo of a number of highly whimsical and experimental contemporary artists who took it a bit too seriously and let themselves go beyond any semblance of 'skill' or even 'concept'. And that's ok, I guess. But let's step back and think about what Johns really meant in this note to himself. What deters you from doing the things that you wish you did or even the things that you *need* to do? The answer for me is usually pretty easy: the big picture. Zooming out too far and thinking about tasks as parts of a large whole or a major achievement makes the tasks feel unachievable, even if they're actually simple.

Sometimes I like to think of my life as a brick house. Disco references be damned, it serves as a pretty good metaphor. Think of a huge meandering castle built of brick. Each individual brick serves a crucial purpose. And yet if you go into the castle and see a single brick laying on the ground, you think, "Oh hell, it's just another pile of bricks." Even a little brick cabin is still just a collection of all its individual components. An architecturally sound and aesthetically appealing structure is created by arranging these components in the most thoughtful, clean and essential form you can. There is no need to go overboard, but we must have a little bit of structure.

Onto the application part of the metaphor: we're unlikely to interpret the *components* of our lives as being as important as our lives at large, when in fact our lives consist *entirely of these components*. You are nothing more than the tiny little moments that fill your day. Each task is not an obstacle but instead an opportunity. Even the most bothersome or even tragic experiences are still opportunities to be handled gently and mindfully.

This is a realization that I believe comes naturally during meditative practice. In focusing on each and every breath, you recognize the simultaneous preciousness and meaninglessness of each moment. Each decision, word, act and intention becomes a mindful opportunity rather than a mindless motion. If you think about being a huge bodybuilder all the time, you'll have more trouble progressing through the hundreds of thousands of reps and exercises that create the ideal physique. If you're obsessed with being rich or famous, you'll neglect the small career decisions and creative advancements that could eventually culminate in wealth or notoriety. If you're fixated on people betraying or offending you, you forget to take the time to win their favor, listen, or show love and compassion. These are all examples of why it is harmful to fixate too much on the future.

Moments are all we have. Focus on the baby steps. They'll run a marathon for you if you let them. I stand by these words with my entire being. I'm not telling anyone to obsess over productivity or become a workaholic. In fact, I want to emphasize the opposite— try to live a life of balanced mindfulness, where each moment has its place. Don't focus on anything but what you can do today. Making the most of each moment will culminate in a life of rewarding spontaneity.

Focus on Details

I know some very intelligent and mindful people who think too big. As kids we were raised to think that we could all be the best at whatever we did, that we could accomplish anything we put our minds to. This sort of hyperbolic ambition might feel good to think about but it can actually deter people from getting anything done. Radio guru Ira Glass said eloquently: "Nobody tells this to people who are beginners, I wish someone told me. All of us who do creative work, we get into it because we have good taste. But there is this gap. For the first couple years you make stuff, it's just not good."

This doesn't just apply to creative work, but to everything. People start with such grand aspirations for what they want to do that they paralyze themselves from ever being able to accomplish *anything* of value for fear of it being bad. The whole idea of "writer's block" is a myth, really. It's just self-consciousness. Anyone can sit and just write if they don't care about the quality of what they're writing. Eventually something materializes. People get so caught up in thoughts and self-judgment that they never sit down and get something going. Picasso said, "Inspiration finds you working."

The Zen mind encourages us to detach from results, expectations and the grand scheme. There are no thoughts. There is no 'greater good'. There's no 'heroic achievement'. There's just the stuff you have to do today. You still need to brush your teeth, make your bed and eat your lunch. Enlightenment is nothing special— that's the point. It is the process of living life simply, essentially, and with mindful diligence. This is why mindfulness and productivity are often correlated, albeit falsely. People who meditate every day train themselves to detach from thoughts, ideals and goals. They can do stuff calmly and methodically without getting bogged down by the big picture. This is productive precisely because it creates people who are unconcerned with productivity.

People today have spoiled life for themselves by caring more about the results than they do the process. Want to know the secret? There are no results. There is *only* the process.

Uncovering Your True Self

It's the nature of organisms on Earth to adapt. Doesn't matter if you're a moth or an advanced mammal; over time you're either going to change or die out. This is basic scientific theory but can be also used metaphorically to understand daily life. The crux of this is that we humans are always adapting, not just on the large scale of base physical or psychological evolution but in the simplest ways in every moment. We adapt to everything. Single people adapt to relationships. Poor people adapt to riches. Rich people adapt to poverty. Nations and races adapt to their geographic locations and environmental conditions. Humans as they exist today vary vastly in appearance and background—the result of millions of years of collective evolution in various environments. On a day-to-day level we are constantly evolving in more nuanced ways. To peer into this process and reflect upon it is to recognize the power of both the individual and the community. How do we collectively foster mindfulness?

Returning to basics: in a very fundamental universal sense, change is the way of the world. There is no moment that is the same as the moment before it. You are a 'different' person at the end of this sentence than you were at the beginning. And yet beneath all of these environmental and sensory changes is your inborn sense of self— this is what I call the spirit. This never changes. It only becomes more or less visible depending on how closely you're paying attention.

The spirit is what exists in every person beneath endless layers of personal experience, conditioning and conceptual chatter. It's your fundamental being. It's also what makes you aware *of* being. And in this sense it *transcends* being. I believe this is the root of religious theories of God and the afterlife. The spirit as felt during meditation and other deep religious experiences is perceived as being above and beyond the self because it is. It doesn't exist in the physical realm and this is precisely what makes it feel so transcendent. Naming it or personifying it does nothing but diminish it. The surface-level beliefs you have about who you are, even down to your family, values and background, are still not who you really are. Underneath all this is a place free of concepts or influence.

This is important to remember when we think about change. When I say that you change in every moment, you may interpret that as some sort of fundamental change. People often refer to their past and say, "I was a different person then." This is only partially true. In reflecting daily on how shallow our interpretations of self often are, we remember not to let these false notions impact our decision process. If someone asks you who you are and your first instinct is to talk about your career, your family or your long-term goals, it's time to dig a bit deeper.

That isn't to say that you should make the conversation all weird and spiritual every time— this is an internal process. It's OK to keep important things to yourself sometimes. There's no need to directly share information about your 'true self'. Merely reflecting within yourself and trying to peel away false layers of identity lets you find a certain peace. This peace will emanate and put others at ease. It will make you more charismatic, since you begin to identify with your deep spiritual self rather than surface-level signifiers. There's no need to communicate the true self directly; it communicates itself through a shift in motivations, actions and thought processes.

Most people treat themselves like a fancy car with a neglected engine— they take care of the surface and maintain appearances but are afraid to pop open the hood and work on what's really important. Meditation is popping open the hood. It lets you see what might initially appear to be "the ugly truth" and then slowly and methodically rid yourself of the grime and gunk that hold you back. It's a degreaser. You are not making yourself different or better. You are just becoming more of who you actually are.

If you choose to meditate regularly, when you think, "Who am I?" you won't say, "I'm a Certified Public Accountant with a 3.8 GPA, $300,000 in the bank, a wife, two kids, 3 cars, a house and a dog," but, simply, "I am." Your essence is who you are stripped of all externals. That doesn't mean you're supposed to throw your material life away and go wander the forest. Some people misinterpret Zen and think they have to become monkish or deny life. I advocate the exact opposite. Live your life fully, work hard, cultivate greatness, do whatever you want, but with this deeper awareness that *you* are fundamentally not anything you do, have, or achieve. You simply are. And, most importantly, recognize that you can only identify with this inner-strength and benevolence to the extent that you're willing to take some time each day to quietly reflect on it. In doing so, you move past shallowness.

This is real adaptation. It's a remedy to most modern problems. It's recognizing your spirit as your center rather than something orbiting around you. How can external orbiting things possibly be your essence? You are your own essence! Misinterpreting this truth is going to cause problems.

Shed Your Ego

"With regard to our whole life, as long as the thing we call "me" does not stop intervening, it is not possible to lead a life that is truly free and peaceful. You already are free, but since you want freedom, you lose it. Consequently, it is necessary to free yourself from thinking that things must be this way or that way. This too is the meaning of the first teaching, "all things are impermanent."
—Sekkei Harada

When you have a free moment, write down all of your problems. Stare at each one and ask the question: where does this come from? Why is this a problem? Whenever I do this, I find that my ego is usually the source of the problem. I live a comfortable life, have a great relationship and have ample free time to spend with my friends or doing things that fulfill me physically and mentally. Still, I get anxiety about random things. Meditation helps me to put life in perspective every day. When I don't do it, I recognize my ego creeping back in.

Meditation practice is precisely that— practice. Even the greatest athletes and performers still need to practice every day. Meditation is a rehearsal for the rest of your time. When you sit and let thoughts come and go without latching onto them, your brain gets controlled practice in non-attachment. Done consistently over a long time, this practice makes you significantly less clingy in daily life. We often associate the word "clingy" with relationships or social situations, but everyone is clingy. We cling to objects, ideas, scenarios and fantasies because they help us get through the day. Meditation helps us realize, however, that clinging to these things simply leads to more clinging. This cycle of attachment represents on a daily level the cycle of samsara, being stuck in the snowball of ego in everyday life.

The more ideas you hold onto, the more you want to keep holding on. The more money you make, the more money you want. And yet beneath every scholar and dolt, every billionaire and bum alike is a single individual human body, a single spirit. We try to evaluate a sense of self based on possessions and externals, but beneath it all is a simple essence that cannot be changed. It differs from person to person and can only be uncovered through conscious reflection.

Working to overcome the ego and uncover the true self has a significant impact on multiple levels. For those who've never taken the time to reflect on the ego and let it subside, uncovering one's true motivations can be a shock. It's incredible the strange webs of delusions people find themselves in when they're too focused on chasing money, appearances, sex, respect, notoriety and all of these things. People end up acting completely irrationally and insane on a daily basis and lose almost all sense of perspective. Those who cultivate mindfulness and reflect find the strength to achieve without identifying with achievement. Sitting in silence and allowing everything to wash over you returns you to the natural state, a state free of culture, ideology or primal desire. It's a state of nothingness that gives the mind space to breathe. As it breathes, it regains control over the toxic ego robot that's holding it hostage. The ego will take as much power as it's granted; most of us give it all our power without even realizing. Even those who believe themselves to be motivated by good intentions are often actually still servants to the ego— those who are charitable as a way of assuaging guilt, those who are kind to others in exchange for social capital, those who work hard just to accumulate things. These are acts of egoism.

Reflection will help you recognize dozens of these acts throughout your day. It may be a rude awakening at first. The truth is painful; that's why lies and deception are so prevalent. Reduction and delusion are the norm; just look around. But recognizing that you have an inner-core of strength and calmness completely revolutionizes your day-to-day life. This core can be cultivated and uncovered more and more. Meditation is the act of getting to know yourself better. Not the ego that you think you are, but your actual deep-down self. This self is more wholesome and more appealing. As you begin to identify more with it and less with the ego, your motivations and actions will shift in a way that will make your life more mindful and meaningful.

The Journey is the Destination

Most of us modern Westerners believe that the path is the path. We're often told linear populist stories on the news, in films, on television and in books that life is fixed, that things happen and then other things happen and if you want to be happy everything's gotta go just like so. If the wrong things happen, it's a problem. Entertainment uses conflict as a plot vehicle; it moves things along. It's a shame we haven't learned from this. Problems are necessary, yet we blow them out of proportion. We cease to realize their impermanence. When it rains, we don't look outside and go, "Oh God no, it's raining! It's never going to stop raining! The world is going to flood over!" We know that it will rain for a fixed period of time and then stop. The rain will have its purpose— it'll wash the streets off, feed the plants and provide sustenance.

Nature always balances this with that. The atoms that comprise the universe are little vibrating balls of conflict and balance, with protons, neutrons and electrons harmonizing one another. It's daytime and then night time. It's summer and then winter. We don't panic thinking that winter will last forever; we have the experience of knowing the snow eventually melts and the warmth emerges. We *know* through experience that summer will come. We have faith in nature to provide us with consistent change. Without destruction, there is no creation. Without darkness, there is no light.

This is where a spiritually harmonious approach to problems comes into the picture. People often reach a period of spiritual seeking after they've had some time in the trenches. I often get notes from readers who've struggled with hard relationships, addiction, violence and other difficult facts of life. The struggles and sufferings of daily life are real. Naturally, they're *at least* half of our experience. They're the night, the rain, the winter, the "negative". But the negative never stands alone. What we perceive as negative has a requisite leveler, the positive. The popular cult of steadfast positivity is garbage because it denies the negative rather than embracing it.

To delve into the realm of corny metaphors, problems are the rain of life. They often disappoint and anger us. But they also enable growth. Without conflict, failure and disruption, there would be no resolution or peace. The obstacle is the path.

The special thing about human perception is that it allows us to regulate the flow of rain, at least to an extent. We rewire our brains to allow the rain just enough time to water the garden without flooding it. The neurotic psyche falls into cyclical thinking patterns when it encounters difficulties. This makes the difficulties even worse. We say too much in arguments, get down on ourselves, and adopt bad habits to cope with stress. These are floods. They are improper reactions to problems that cause more problems and throw things out of balance. Through meditation we discover a mindful approach to distress. Instead of feeding the fire, we let it slowly fade away, in the same way that we let thoughts come and go during the practice itself. We don't deny the existence of obstacles, but we approach them in a constructive way and recognize them as balanced elements of an unpredictable path.

Wanting, Needing and Having

"If you chase two rabbits you will catch neither."
—*Russian proverb*

The most common debate I have with myself is over this whole dichotomy of attachment and nonattachment. I practice Zen meditation every day but I don't consider myself a Buddhist. The idea that attachment is the root of all suffering and that the goal of life should be to find a way to relieve this suffering is stupid to me. I find value in suffering and attachment. To deny attachment and deny suffering is avoidant; it's a denial of life itself. In dealing with pain properly, one cultivates strength— the strength required to withstand more pain and overcome more difficulty. The process never ends, it just grows more nuanced.

This is why I've been drawn Zen since I was a kid. It doesn't focus quite so much on the feel-good life-denial parts of Buddhism but instead on the abstract realism of the Tao and simply being present in every moment of experience. It's a sort of benign lucidity in everything. In the meditative state one is both blissfully unaware and brilliantly aware of everything. Still, Zazen is difficult. It hurts. It *causes* a certain degree of physical suffering to the uninitiated. It also confronts the scattered modern mind with plenty of emotional challenges. Dealing with buried emotions and ideas is hard work, but of course it's worth suffering over. Meditation has taught me that suffering is a crucial part of life, not something to be overcome. We can't avoid attachment. It's simply impossible, even in complete monastic seclusion. To yearn for an avoidance of attachment is as strong an attachment as any other. As such, we have to learn how to function not without attachment, but instead floating somewhat above it. This is what meditation helps me do.

Internally I like to break it down into three states: needing, wanting and having. Clinging comes from wanting and not having. Confusion comes from having and not wanting. Contentment comes from not wanting and not having and not *needing*. In many cases, wisdom comes from recognizing the specific things that one neither haves nor wants, and avoiding them. Lastly, it's important to recognize the things one has that one *does* want. The former is the art of simplicity, the latter the art of gratitude. Wisdom similarly comes from recognizing the difference between needing and wanting and eliminating harmful wants. These simple realizations are some of the greatest *practical* gifts I've found in Zen practice. I love the stories of vagabond masters who were content to beg, climb mountains, pick flowers, write poetry, drink rice wine and teach kids how to meditate.

Instead of attaching to unattainable ideals and silly abstract concepts, we should find beauty in what surrounds us no matter where we are. We should always live simply. We can train ourselves to deeply want what we already have and can never lose, thus appreciating it in perpetuity.

This is why I often say that the good life is as simple as paying attention. I know lots of miserable rich people and contented poor people. The goal is to reorient your attention and recognize the true dynamics of wanting and having. In doing so we get rid of the unessential and devote more energy to feeling blessed with the simple things in life. From this foundation, we grow towards being able to healthily live with whatever comes along.

Let Your Thoughts Go

"No sooner does a man know the reason of a thing than immediately he tires of it and goes casting about for something new." —Meister Eckhart

A major lesson of meditation is understanding impermanence. Something about the process of reflection allows people to recognize the fleeting nature of everything. In Zen, there's a saying— let your thoughts come and go, but don't serve them tea. When you sit in reflection for a dedicated period each day, patterns of thought begin to emerge. You recognize that these thoughts come and stay a while. They may even try to overstay. But eventually they *all* leave, no matter what. Over time, this self-honesty cultivates an inner-strength and peace of mind. Good thoughts or bad, none of them are here to stay. Your sense of self and perception is always in a state of flux.

You only really build recognition of this when you see it happen yourself. Occasionally I'll be meditating and a really pressing thought will come into my head. If it's extremely important, I'll take pause and write it down. The filmmaker David Lynch said many of his best creative ideas come to him during meditation. He compares it to going deep into the sea to find the biggest fish. But most of the time I will sit through the thought. We are not meditating to find good ideas. Most of the thoughts, by virtue of averages, are unimportant clutter. If I find myself indulging in them or giving them attention, I will withdraw and let them shrink into the abyss. Meditation teaches you the art of neutral observation.

This symbolically carries over into other parts of life, and this is where the commonly discussed 'benefits' of meditation come from. When you learn not to indulge in your thoughts, you learn not to indulge in other things. The voice in your head slowly morphs from an ego voice into a neutral higher spiritual voice. For me, this voice has become an authority in my life; it's the voice of my true nature. It represents a heightened awareness that my ego self is not so quick to understand. It reminds me to refrain from self-destructive habits. It reminds me to be grateful. It reminds me to tell my girlfriend I love her and to treat my family with respect. It helps me live a more virtuous life. From the greatest spiritual questions to the smallest daily trivialities, the mindful voice guides you through life. Meditation refines this voice.

This is most important in the realm of patience and attachment. When the brain trains itself not to take its thoughts too seriously, not to dive into the depths of pessimism or get lost in the delusion of optimism, you find a certain type of objectivity.

Instead of latching on to material thirsts and overambitious goals, the meditative mind tells you to simply focus on what you have to do today. Over long periods of time, this lets you accomplish great things. As Lao Tzu said, "The world is won by those who let it go."

When you find yourself feeling hateful or angry, the meditative mind starts an internal dialog. It says, "What's the point? Your hate or anger may be rooted in reality, but getting upset about things that are outside of your control doesn't do anyone any good." This is supremely helpful. It also cultivates growth on a deeper spiritual level. Instead of taking your thoughts at face value, you always approach the ego mind with a degree of heightened caution.

Lastly, the meditative mind knows to be contented with what it has. That doesn't mean that it becomes lazy or static, but instead that it simply knows how to express gratitude. When you slow down and really think about who you are and what your life is, you will find plenty to be grateful for. You may have problems, but there's always a balance. There are always experiences to cherish: time with loved ones, time in nature, quiet moments of contemplation. Even our sufferings can be beautiful if we recognize them as learning opportunities. The meditative mind has the patience to let the dust clear and recognize the inherent duality of everything.

Be the Calm

I see many well-intentioned people imploring others to "be the change they wish to see in the world". This is a now-classic spiritual cliché, which I believe was originally popularized by Gandhi. Simply put, I think it's dangerous and unnecessary. Most people are not ready to try to change the world, nor do they have the tools required to make any valuable impact. Those who try are often met by nature's intense retaliation. So what can we do?

We should start by focusing on the idea of becoming *calm*. In doing this, we access a more honest place within ourselves and cultivate inner-strength. What results is a more comprehensive way of approaching the world that, through personal transformation and ever-increasing degrees of self-discipline, results in constructive change by default.

To be change is simply to become chaos, especially in a world that is already always in natural flux. To obsess over change is to be perpetually dissatisfied. It is to act, not necessarily on the best judgment, but instead on the mere desire to make things different from how they are. Why do we do this? It rarely solves anything.

This is the strange paradox about this cultural idea of progress; it relies on a continual process of tearing down just so new structures can be built over the rubble. It is a destructive impulse. The stronger the impulse for change, the more severe the destruction that ensues. The supreme irony is that those who are unwilling to change themselves often try to change the world to meet their needs. Who's more in control here? True change comes from within. If you cannot be the calm, you cannot be the change.

There is no change without the calm. In fact, the most revolutionary change today would be to embrace the calm, to fall backwards into a simpler and more humble state. We destroy ourselves more and more every time we forcefully accelerate towards the next change. Think of how many people who try to change the world just act hastily and make things worse. They look to the external world as a solution to their problems.

Zen implores us to do the reverse. Correct your internal state, and the world will benefit. Slow down and life becomes clearer. When we are so focused on what's next we miss the moment and lose sight of how to make life meaningful.

You Make You Happy

Materialism is often perceived as a mere obsession with money. It's more than this. Materialism manifests in a variety of ways, the most subtle of which lead people towards unnecessary suffering. It's natural for people to search for contentment in external circumstances. The truth of the matter, unfortunately, is that contentment can never be found in material circumstances alone.

When you set a goal and achieve it, you may experience happiness. That happiness comes from you, not the goal. The achievement is simply a conduit for the happiness. In attaching yourself to things like this, you trick your brain into experiencing contentment when you get those things. The problem with this is that it sets up a cycle of perpetual dissatisfaction. When you want something and reward yourself for getting it, you are effectively training yourself to just keep wanting more. You then end up having to force yourself to jump through countless hoops just to 'get your fix'.

This is a simple concept and yet most people don't seem to recognize it. Many spend their entire lives chasing achievements, material goods, fantasies, relationships and ideals, all while never recognizing that the satisfaction they feel in achieving these things is accessible within. Not only this— it *comes* from within, and only within.

Recognizing this is a wonderful opportunity to simplify your life. Most of the things you chase in the day-to-day only make you happy to the extent that you are capable of making yourself happy in response to their attainment. If you cut out the unnecessary middleman and learn to simply do things that *reveal* this preexistent inner-contentment and peace, you're effectively beating the system. The game of life becomes profoundly easier when you recognize that all the satisfaction you could ever need is within you.

Imagine if someone walked up to you right now and gave you a check for a billion dollars. That would 'change your life', wouldn't it? It would reorient your priorities. You would have all of your material worries figured out forever. Try to really put yourself into this mindset. Your circumstances would change, but you yourself wouldn't change one bit. You would still look the same. You would still have had the same upbringing. Your thought patterns would still function in the same way.

This sort of visualization is important, not the rags-to-riches visualization, but instead the recognition that no matter how much your external circumstances change, you fundamentally remain the same. You are the master of your domain. You can achieve all of your wildest dreams and feel no better about yourself than you do right now. Many a 'successful' person has spoken about this. Why do you think so many rich and famous people are drawn to meditation? People achieve their wildest dreams and realize that they are no more contented than before, precisely because they were willing to forego contentment in order to achieve those dreams.

The key is to recognize that chasing external circumstances is not the answer. That is simply a distraction from the present moment, in which you must always confront yourself. Meditation is often so difficult for people because it forces them to confront years of lies and self-deception. It brings everything to the surface. It's like looking into a high-magnification mirror and seeing your blemishes for the first time.

Over time, reflecting on yourself proves more valuable for well-being than chasing the external world. Reflection allows you the opportunity to make good with yourself, to recognize who you truly are. In doing this, you bypass the need to constantly be distracting yourself with rewards, punishments and achievements. Finding peace within, external stuff becomes less important to us.

For most people today, this subtle shift in mindset changes life completely. People rarely take a second to recognize their motivations or see the roots of their desires. They simply do what they're used to. In engaging in a consistent process of reflection, they recognize that they are who they are, and that no achievement and no amount of money will change who they are.

This makes people content with what they have but also primes them for a life of healthy 'success' should they achieve even their wildest goals. A person who is content with little is best at being successful, since they recognize that their self worth is not dependent on any notion of external wealth. They can live with or without success and they don't pretend that the source of contentment is in wealth or achievement exclusively. The person who reflects recognizes the important relationship between the inner and outer self, and the inner and outer world. The more you ponder this relationship and cultivate inner-strength, the better equipped you will be to handle whatever the material world throws at you.

Thoughts Have No Power

A simple lesson of meditation is that your thoughts do not actually have any definitive power over you. *You* have power over you. When your hold over yourself is weak, or your understanding of what we call the 'true self' is underdeveloped, thoughts often come in and take over. They convince you that they are in charge.

This is why people experience a shift in perspective after even just a few weeks or months of daily meditation practice. They begin to regain control over their thoughts. Thoughts belong to you. You are in charge of them, not the other way around. When you practice letting them come and go in a controlled setting, you remind yourself of your control. Your feelings of helplessness and self-pity cease and you finally recognize that you are in charge of how you think and feel.

In meditation, we focus on breath and posture not because they are formalities but in order to direct the mind towards inner focus rather than outer focus. Thoughts are what connect us to the world, but all thoughts are 'tainted' with the falseness of cognition. What do I mean by this? Zen masters speak of pure experience— that microscopic moment we experience *before* we think about what we've experienced. That is the place beyond judgment, the truth, the real. That lack of judgment is what we achieve during meditation when we are patient enough.

How does this carry into everyday life? It permeates every waking moment, decision and mental faculty. When you reflect on thoughts during meditation, you start to see how they spread mimetically. One thought becomes two, those two become four, those four become sixteen, etc. The tangential relationships between ideas often drown us in anxiety. Similarly, when we act we are often bogged down by thoughts and can't make proper decisions. Samurai used to train themselves to be able to make decisions without thinking twice, lest their actions become diluted by false conceptualization.

The meditative mind trusts its gut not as an impulsive reaction, but instead as a rational and effective source of pre-cognitive decision making. Deep down, you know what to do. You just haven't uncovered confidence in this ability yet. Meditation will teach you this confidence.

Infinite Gratitude

There seem to be endless narratives surrounding what makes life happy, meaningful, contented, full, etc. Our values, actions and thoughts often vary based on how we relate to these concepts and which we prioritize over others. These prioritizations themselves also vary greatly and know few cultural, geographic or religious bounds. In this globalized life of simultaneous intense inter-connectedness and isolation, we're on our own in how we perceive the world. You may feel alone in how you experience your unique confluence of individual ideas, but you are also freer than ever to engineer your own way of working with these ideas.

Someone may prioritize happiness, for example, but cling to their ideal state so intensely that they cease to recognize happiness in the moment. Or maybe they yearn for contentment so much that the inevitable lack of it makes them uneasy— a sure formula for perpetual discontent. Or perhaps they search day and night for meaning in books, conversations and experiences, only to find themselves constantly hoping for the next thing.

The common thread among everything ailing us is clinging. We only feel loss when we cling. We only feel disappointment when we expect. We only feel neediness or yearning in response to a sense of lack. Much of what we yearn for is a fantasy. These fantasies often hold us back and prevent us from fully experiencing the infinitude of the present moment. We yearn more for the fantasy than we do the object of it. Reality can be difficult to face, but when faced with grace the opportunities to see love and beauty are infinite.

With each passing day there's a choice— be grateful or be greedy. The more we thirst for more, the less content we are with what we have. But in stepping back and recognizing all the gifts of life, from the smallest details to the grandest ideals, we find so many magnificent wonders to think about. There's only so much time each day to think. It's better spent contemplating benevolence and gratitude than it is mulling over the tiny evils and lacking facets of your life.

Now we enter the state of gratitude. This state doesn't mean that everything is OK. There's always room for growth and new understanding. Sometimes we just feel outright bad, and that's alright. But the state of gratitude is that in which we recognize our blessings and really understand why they're blessings. This is more an emotional state than a rational thinking state. Resorting to this in times of suffering rather than indulging in self-loathing and outward hatred is a crucial decision that completely changes the way we approach life.

It's OK to let yourself go a bit. Prayer and meditation aren't about willing desires into being or making new things happen, but about reflecting upon what is. The more fully and beautifully we can experience what is, the better equipped we will be to embrace what life has to offer. In focusing on the present, you allow for the fullest and most contented future. In being grateful, you recognize that you have everything you need.

The Truth is Where You Are

"If you cannot find the truth right where you are, where else do you expect to find it?"— Dōgen

Wherever you are right now, take a short break from reading this. Close your eyes and take a breath. Don't force the breath. Just focus on its natural movement. Do this ten times. Then open your eyes and return to what you were doing.

When we take a step back and embody the meditative mindset, we can recognize the present moment as all there is. It's all there ever will be. Everything about the future is speculation, everything about the past mere remembrance. We can rely on all of these conceptualizations to get things done in the 'real world', but they harm us as soon as they prevent us from being able to step back and enter into the present moment. This inability prevents us from living fully, even if there are things we are scared to confront.

This is the impact of Zen practice— it allows us to step back at will. In a sense, this immersion into each moment is less a stepping back and more a diving in. When you recognize every moment as an infinitude unto itself, you feel rather compelled to dive in. Sometimes you even feel a responsibility to. It's like diving into a spring of eternal life and eternal peace. There's no anxiety, no analysis, no happiness nor sadness. It's a space of pure contemplation.

The cliché goes, "Treat every day as if it is your last. One day you will be right." That's cute, and it's a good mindset— but what does this really mean? I would go one step further and say to treat every tiny moment as if it is your last. This is true Zen mind. When you treat life in this way, you never take anything for granted. You discover things you never would have seen in a state of mindless attachment. It's so simple— the way towards better vision is just to look closer.

That said, there's no calm without occasional chaos. Distractions run rampant and there are always self-imposed challenges in discovering the way. These challenges shouldn't be resisted but instead welcomed with open arms. Carl Jung said, "What resists persists." The meditative mind lets every thought come and go. The periods of quiet in which thoughts stop appearing are what we call samadhi: pure focus. These moments are really special, but they are also nothing special. They only come about when we stop treating meditation as something special. Similarly, thoughts only subside when we stop thinking about thoughts.

Look at Nothing

Ten minutes or so into my daily meditation practice, I sometimes hit a certain apex. Though my eyes are closed, the world around me feels as if it is sinking into itself. I begin to feel enlarged and spread out, and my focus level peaks. It's difficult to get tired at this point. The tiredness tends to come a few minutes later. I like to think of this as a period of intense awareness in which my brain is reconnecting with nothingness.

If you participate in the modern world, your attention is spread too thin. We all have to deal with this to varying extents. There's no way to operate optimally and work within society without spreading ourselves too thin. It's simply the way of the world. To deny it is to deny oneself a sense of participation in life, so we should work with what we have. Not everyone can give it all up for the Ashram, and that's ok. The greatest masters believed that practice is meant for the real world, not the temples.

For me, the way of coping with this is taking some time each day to soberly stare into the void. Meditation is precisely this. It allows me the chance to close my eyes, cross my legs, remove as much sensory stimuli as possible, and exist purely and honestly for a brief period each day. It's funny that this is a necessary requisite for coping with an inorganic and chaotic world, but we don't need to look at meditation this way. People were meditating long before iPhones.

Meditation has the metaphorical significance of providing an internal backdrop for thinking about infinitude. In the same way you feel as if you're gazing into the infinite while looking at stars from a field, you get this impression after a few minutes of eyes-closed upright breathing. The effect is quite similar. Extended into the material realm, we ponder the relationship between inner-space and outer-space. Neither have been fully explained or conquered by science nor religion; one could argue they are so essential and intangible that they are by nature unconquerable.

This is the importance of looking at nothing; it's effectively a way of looking at everything. Out there, in the material world, you're so distracted and distraught. Your attention hangs in the balance between past, present, and future. It has no choice but to constantly jump around and catch various diversions in its huge net. There's work to be done, people to be dealt with, problems to solve. All of these problems fade away after you get acquainted a bit with nothingness. Oddly, instead of this causing us to get lazy or give things up, it provides the mind with just the peaceful balance it needs to retain its sense of dignity and respect.

If there's anything we have trouble accessing, it's a self-directed sense of respect. People abuse their bodies with food, drugs, alcohol, stress and laziness. They abuse their minds with dramatic simulations of death and degeneracy. Popular culture has developed in such a way that these vices have only become more appealing and potent over time; they are irresistible to most. These delivery systems are engineered to access your monkey mind, the mind fixated on the most base material activities and thoughts. And they work! People spend a large part of the day behaving like mindless apes. What can we do to halt this collective regression?

If entertainment can be said to lower the mind's attention, meditation raises it back up again. By balancing out the chaos with some peace and quiet, the brain reclaims its deep ancient powers of contemplation. This is why some people today find such incredible solace in meditation— it brings them back to their spiritually-wired brain, a brain neglected for years in favor of flashy signals. We don't meditate to be more productive or make more money, but instead to reclaim our humanity.

Invest in the Present

A lot of people aren't aware that meditation can be rather painful at times. You hear plenty about the benefits of meditation, because writing about these benefits spurs clicks and popular consciousness. People love to think a simple practice will serve as a cure-all for their problems. Based on my experience, the number of people who speak of the benefits of meditation and the number of people who actually practice every day are significantly different. I don't make much money from Daily Zen, so I have no reason to pander to you and tell you that meditation is all butterflies and puppy dogs. It's actually pretty difficult. It's not for everyone, but if you commit to meditation against your indulgent comfort instinct, it will make you into someone who can handle it. Subsequently, it will make you into someone who can handle other risks and discomforts. That's a transformative gift to give yourself. You are recognizing your strength.

The first time I sat in meditation for thirty minutes, I experienced some intense physical pain. My legs fell asleep and then became stiff. My back became tense and felt like it was going to spasm. Contrary to the image of meditation as a comfy-cozy form of blissing out, this was hard work.

This physical pain can also be accompanied by a test of will that, at time, borders on mental pain. Think about how distracted your mind is. How often do you check your phone in a day? Your email? How many intrusive thoughts keep you from getting stuff done? How many times do you think about sex? What about food? How many times do you get angry? There are thousands of distractions in this world. Going from 100 to 0 can really send you into a state of confusion. You'll be amazed by how often your ego-driven mind tries to convince you to stop meditating. The mind wants to ignore its inner-stillness so badly. Meditation is hard for beginners precisely for this reason.

Have I turned you off yet? Oops. But those more mindful readers, even those who don't meditate, will recognize an opportunity here. Part of the value of meditative practice is sticking with it. Over time, the physical pain subsides. The mental pain subsides. Even if you find yourself distracted at times, these distractions are often punctuated by profound moments of illumination. I love those moments. And I love the consistency of meditation practice. My chaotic mind yearns for a chance to examine its own peaceful roots once a day for a short period of time.

Let's think about what 'investment' means. An investment is a controlled allocation of resources that, because of the control part, increases in value over time. Instead of eating a $20 lunch every day, you cook and bag a lunch for $5. You save $15 a day. A year goes by, and you have saved roughly $5500. This appreciates over time. Thanks to compound interest, years later, your self-control puts your kids through school or something. I like to think of the benefits of healthy habits as a form of compound interest. Meditation might be tough at first. Over time, though, the consistency builds upon itself and its value multiplies. The initial difficulty ends up allowing you to live a life of contentment and mindfulness— definitely a good trade. Similarly, exercise hurts. Getting up to lift weights or run at 6am is trying at first. But seeing the sunrise, feeling your body alive and breathing, losing weight and feeling good about yourself in exchange for a little bit of pain and sacrifice each day? Yes, please. That's what pain is for— you trade it in for greatness and self-respect. It's an abstract form of investment.

The point here is that, within reason, pain is a good thing. Most of what people shirk from in daily life is not life-threatening. We are creatures of comfort. We do what feels good and what is easy. Those who go out of their way to take risks and do things that frighten them often reap huge rewards. As many a master meditator will tell you, though, the reward is in the act itself. The journey is the destination. Once you internalize this, you'll have no problem making consistent investments in the present. Over time, they flourish beautifully.

Finding Emptiness

"Emptiness which is conceptually liable to be mistaken for sheer nothingness is in fact the reservoir of infinite possibilities." — D.T. Suzuki

"Thirty spokes share the wheel's hub;
It is the center hole that makes it useful.
Shape clay into a vessel;
It is the space within that makes it useful.
Cut doors and windows for a room;
It is the holes which make it useful.
Therefore profit comes from what is there;
Usefulness from what is not there."
—Tao Te Ching

The Western mind tends to have a really hard time adapting to some of the most important concepts in Zen. To many it seems like a nonsensical framework. As a result, the type of Zen that is usually sold to large audiences is not Zen at all, but a sort-of goal-oriented New Age spirituality labeled as Zen. It is much easier to read a few books than it is to commit yourself to sitting in meditation every day. Meditating every day requires a discipline that many people find impossible to cultivate. Those who do are continually surprised by just how transformative the meditative mind is.

The passage here from the Tao Te Ching functions on a few levels. In spiritual literature, humans are often referred to as "vessels" for divine energy. Outside of a religious context, we can view people as vessels for all types of energy. The way people choose to live determines what sort of energy they absorb. Much like forming the wad of clay into a bowl, meditation forms the mind into a receptive spiritual vessel. The experience of the meditative mind is not the experience of nothingness, like Suzuki says, but the experience of emptiness. From this emptiness comes the usefulness of the mind. In focusing on emptiness and uselessness, we find the most profound usefulness.

Your mind can't do its job if it's filled with inflexible thoughts and judgments. A degree of emptiness is required to let thoughts come and go without letting them rot. Meditation encourages this flow of ideas. Metaphorically, the in and out movements of the breath provide a framework by which thoughts flow in and out, too. Allowing everything to come and go without latching on, as we all do to varying degrees, totally changes our relationships with events, ideas, people and things.

Thoughts also need space to float around. Study must always be balanced with experience. Have you ever spoken to someone who only reads books all day? They're often lost in their own heads and full of information they don't know what to do with. Those who don't study or pontificate at all and live life exclusively through experience are often similarly one-dimensional. Countless great scholars and mystics throughout history have praised a balance between work and life, study and experience, wisdom and knowledge.

In the chaotic modern world, a mid-day meditation session can be just the balance one needs. Amidst constant sensory input, calls for productivity and creativity, and desires of yourself and others, some time to simply sit in quietude can reinvigorate the mind. Mindless activities bunch you up into a clay ball; meditation expands and shapes you gracefully into a vessel for spiritual energy, love, self-discipline and diligence.

Enter the Spirit Realm

It doesn't require an expert to look at modern culture and recognize just how self-indulgent it is. When so many large businesses rely on advertising to boost success, and mass-media is more effective and invasive than ever, advertising becomes an all-out assault on human sensibilities. Every inborn desire and necessity is exploited for maximum gain. Even if you don't buy lots of stuff, your senses are constantly bombarded by attempts to convince you to.

This is to say that most of us live in a climate of chaotic sensory input. We're distracted. Our minds are full of junk, and we lack self-discipline. Literacy may be at an all-time high, yet 42% of college graduates never read another book. Fancy gyms, diets, and fad workouts may seemingly be more popular than ever, but 36% of adults are considered obese. Meanwhile, humans have spent so long shirking from reality that they seem to think virtual reality might be a better idea. In other words, this nebulous globalized culture obsessed with individual pleasure and perspective has lost its sense of self-discipline. With our historical lack of piety or discipline has come freedom of mind and freedom to squander it on distractions.

Don't stop reading. There's some good news. Individualism has made it easier than ever to do your own thing. Even if most people use this cultural individualism as an excuse to be self-indulgent and leisurely, you still have all the resources at your disposal to attempt to break free at any time. You have access to every book ever written. You have free immediate access to methods by which you can survive and make a living from anywhere in the world. With full autonomy and individual agency comes the option to work really hard and make the most of your circumstances. This is a truly beautiful thing, and it's always open to self-motivated individuals.

The crux of living on your own terms is not indulging in every hedonistic whim like remnant 60's bohemian fantasies, but instead simplifying. Zen teaches true students to recognize all that is delusional and unnecessary, and cut it out slowly and deliberately like surgeon carefully removes a malignant growth. For this reason, it has always been a self-selected movement. Throughout history, the vast majority of people have always done as they are told, followed trends and created mass culture. Always. That's why it's called "mass" culture! Certain types of people become fed up with this nonsense and decide to stop directing their attention outward. They instead direct it inward, and discover the beauty of self-sufficiency, and spiritual living. Every mystical religious tradition in history is born of this impulse.

Meditation is difficult. For the perpetually distracted person, it sometimes feels nearly impossible. But as I've said a million times, this difficulty is why it's so important. Meditation is such a simple act and yet it slowly and steadily reverses all of this distracted conditioning and brings us back to a peaceful place thousands of years old, a place of calmness and stillness where the deepest recesses of your spirit reside. When you first encounter this stillness, you feel as if it's been waiting for you your whole life. You feel truly blessed to have discovered it.

Sitting in this place allows you to reflect, to see yourself as you really are and to recognize the world for what it really is. If you visit this place daily and spend some quality time there, your entire perspective begins to change. Meditation is like a daily vacation to the spirit-realm. It might not be easy or immediately gratifying, but this is what makes it so rewarding. I ask that you give it a chance and keep your expectations low. Your expectations and ego are what set you back and keep you in the world of distracted chaos. Meditation teaches you to transcend them and to exist above everything that's merely material and conceptual. It completely reorients your way of being and thinking.

No Mud, No Lotus

This catchy title is from the eponymous Thich Nhat Hanh book. It's an excellent book that uses simple language to explore how we must embrace both what we judge as "good" and "bad" in order to grow mindfully. This is a classic Zen concept— we embrace both sides of a duality and transcend them to arrive at a better place.

Western philosophy has always struggled to recognize this transcendence and has often been bogged down by dualism in favor of practicality and logical soundness. Even the groundbreaking work of Hegel sought to reconcile one side of an argument's 'thesis' with the other side, 'antithesis', thus creating a bonded connection between the two, a 'synthesis'. This allows not for a transcendence of dualism but instead for a further entrenchment in it. As such, instead of moving past opposing concepts, Westerners have just combined them into more complicated workings— often at the expense of their sanity.

Similarly, I believe lovingkindness type thinkers like Thich Nhat Hanh also miss the mark. Maybe I'm cynical; I don't think any Zen master can reach such a massive audience without dumbing things down a bit, but...

"Both suffering and happiness are of an organic nature, which means they are both transitory; they are always changing. The flower, when it wilts, becomes the compost. The compost can help grow a flower again. Happiness is also organic and impermanent by nature. It can become suffering and suffering can become happiness again." (No Mud, No Lotus)

I love Zen precisely because of this sort of simplicity. But I think this approach combined with the more vexing considerations that old-school Zen masters brought into their teachings is important. Hanh relies too heavily on the idea of happiness, an experience that in other writings he advises readers to transcend in favor of inner-peace. Sort-of like the way Hegelian thinkers can never let go of the original thesis or antithesis and are forced to make a compromise between the lesser elements of each, Hanh isn't inviting us to embrace suffering unconditionally and find peace. He's saying "if you just cradle and nurture your suffering with compassion for yourself you will eventually experience happiness."

The way towards peace is not to endure suffering with the knowledge that it's the other side of happiness. The true way is to sit through both and come out the other side having truly moved beyond both suffering and happiness. Why waste more time embracing suffering in order to just keep chasing happiness? I feel meditation really helps me move beyond both, not to a point of synthesis, compromise, or even contradiction, but to a realm of neutral peaceful experience. This is the beautiful 'interzone' in which the flower is simultaneously the dirt. It's all the same.

When I'm in a political mood I like to think of the meditating mind as Switzerland. Switzerland is still a strong nation despite having been a completely neutral country— they haven't fought a war since signing the Treaty of Paris in 1815. That's enough time to dispel certain myths that a country can't be internally strong, peaceful and isolationist and still survive. Our American mindset often mirrors our policies— we're obsessed with material things, exploitation, individuality, fairness, happiness and freedom, and we're always getting all up in other people's business to prove it even if we don't have a good reason or a good mind. When you sit, you slowly transition into a neutral state.

Yes, it's true that without the mud there's no flower. But we start to misunderstand Zen as soon as we perceive the mud and the flower in opposition. In fact, they're in cahoots. They're working together with reasonless reason and purposeless purpose. Such is the way of nature. Things happen the way they happen. We can jump on board and embrace this harmonious spirit or risk being thrust into a world of chaos and conflict. The peaceful life is one in which we acknowledge that 'happiness' and 'suffering' are made up. They're all in your head. There's no need to focus on either or both. In simple practice and simple action we find the peaceful place beyond concepts.

Go Beyond Logic

"By letting it go it all gets done.
The world is won by those who let it go.
But when you try and try,
The world is beyond the winning."
— Lao Tzu

Letting go isn't easy. Our world preaches the goodness of the hunt, the quest, the journey— but only with a destination. The journey without a destination is of no interest, for we seem to not qualify anything as a journey if it doesn't have some sort of purpose. The irony ends up being that we're always living for the next checkpoint or achievement. We're artificially adapting towards being unable to smell the roses. All quandaries and interpretations lose their nuance as soon as they're quantified. We live lives of increased quantification, and yet numbers do not mean anything outside of the human realm. They merely represent abstract processes in nature that we've managed to pin down with symbols. But where does this all come from? Why are humans so bent on projecting a cloudy will of control onto an uncaring world despite rarely ever possessing the discipline to do so on a spiritual level?

The answer is fear. We do not like nature's seeming purposelessness. Newer generations are conditioned less and less to cope with nature; it does not function like technology. Some of the smartest humans have used science as a crutch to replace the massive spiritual void of the post-Industrial age. As nature continues about its business, increasingly at odds with a humanity that has, by choice, given up on trying to make peace with its inevitable mystery, humans are holding on with a tighter grip.

There's no use doing most of what we do if we can't set some time aside for spiritual practice. Trying to apply advanced science to a population of anti-intellectual anti-spiritual dolts is like trying to put jet fuel in a go-kart. This is where the principle of letting go becomes so important. We have to let go of our fear of the irrational and especially of the post-rational. Nature is not rational. Science is rational because it has projected itself onto nature to explain and emulate natural processes, but this rationality does not reflect the true process of nature. Because of its basis in rationality, science can never replicate nature, it can only imitate it. Humans can rise above this suicidal limitation of scientific rationality through a true embrace of nature and spiritual reflection. Find the place beyond logic where the truth sits around and waits. It doesn't get many visitors these days.

Educate Yourself

"The most popular hostess at a nightclub might think proudly, "I'm number one." However, she sometimes feels loneliness and emptiness within this favorable condition because she finds that she's simply the most expensive commodity for sale in the store's showcase. No matter how expensively she's sold, the moment she discovers deep in her mind that she's just a commodity, she'll naturally feel empty." —Kosho Uchiyama

Schools teach children the importance of high performance. The subject matter itself is often less important than the opportunity it provides for a high score. Standardized testing is important in the career of most students, and yet it relies on a machine-graded system. The questions, by their very nature, cannot contain much nuance or natural intrigue. They can rely on trickery, sure, but at the end of each one the student still has to circle an answer— and quickly.

On a symbolic level, what does this do to the young mind? Thinking back to my days as a Standardized Student, I can recall the sort of mindset one must put oneself in to accomplish the feat of a standardized test. It is an inhuman mode, a machine mode. The studying process requires one to treat the mind like a computer. It dwells in internal scripts like this:

This is the information. I am acquiring it. The test will challenge my skill in information acquisition. I will either choose the correct answer or the incorrect answer. If I choose the incorrect answer, I risk getting a low score. If I get a low score, I will appear inferior to my competitor. I will potentially be rejected from a prestigious institution. If I am rejected from a prestigious institution, I will have less of a chance of getting a secure job. Better choose the correct answer.

Interesting to see how this thought process ends up mirroring the inane machinery of the modern world— cause and effect, cause and effect, cause and effect. Everything is done like a Bobby Fischer chess play, planning 40 moves in advance to crush what is in this case a paper tiger.

One more point of contention: it makes sense, of course, that such an educational system is engineered on a bell curve. The test is pre-tested on focus groups to make sure that the mean score will always be distributed towards the center, setting a standard for rote normality. In other words, it guarantees the majority of participants will achieve mediocre scores. It's engineered to do so! When you're systematically rewiring human brains to be like rats in a cheese maze, you can do things like this. I see this sort of engineering as symbolic of what has happened in society as a whole, and what we should aim to overcome through our practice.

An educational system designed in this way, with these effects, has a spiritual impact on millions of young people. It maps an existing and cemented industrial system of competition, materialism, and forced mediocrity and projects it back upon the new generation, thus inducting them into the system. It is an artificial initiation process for humans. It's unnatural. Why else would more than 10% of teens abuse stimulants prescribed for ADHD? We are born into a system that has evolved far beyond our own interests, and yet young people often have no choice but to join. The consequences of dropping out seem too grave.

It's unlikely that such an approach to education will change in the near future. It supports a system of industry that is too profitable to slow down; objects in motion tend to stay in motion until they crash and burn. There will certainly be a rupture at some point, but our energy is better spent educating ourselves than trying to take down a massive machine.

Why is self education important? It's important because we're all the vain nightclub hostess described by master Uchiyama. Throughout our participation in the cycle of materialism, we find our skills only within the system itself. We're rewarded for them and told we're special. The artist gets a job as a product photographer. The writer gets a job as a sponsored content writer. The musician sells a beat or a jingle for 5 grand here and there. The entrepreneur is forced to make concessions, to appeal to a masses that have been rigged from childhood towards the bell curve of mediocrity. This sets the bar lower and lower over time. It leaves most people feeling empty, regardless of whether or not they have the reflective capacity to realize it! This is why Zazen is so crucial.

The way towards self-education is not just to read books. This is, of course, deeply important. A life spent reading and experiencing the perspectives of others is priceless. But on top of this, Zen practice helps us regain a true sense of self, one unencumbered by the false expectations of robots. This allows us to hold ourselves to even higher standards than those promoted by modern education, long forgotten standards in the realm of the masses: virtue, compassion, honor, reliability, consistency, respect, discipline and humility.

A reflective type of self-education allows us to live in an entirely different realm from those stuck in the daily machinery of cause and effect. I mentioned this concept briefly in a prior chapter. Basically, the cycle of samsara exists as modern society itself. This cycle contains all the vapid striving of the world and all these ideological problems. Most people are stuck in the cycle of intellectual samsara. Through shifting our values towards those previously mentioned, we slowly and steadily rise about this cycle. We return to nature. We dive off the sinking ship of the modern world and swim to the shore.

Resist Infectious Negativity

"Darkness and light to you are both alike."
(Ps. 139:12)

Seeing as we are in and of the natural world, it makes sense that a vast number of metaphors for human experience are reflected within nature. Things that are brought into form, whether by will or by accident, tend to multiply. Organisms reproduce. "Objects in motion tend to stay at motion." Let us then think about the concept of benevolence. I equate goodness with calmness and indifference, like the Chinese concept of Wu-Wei— action through non-action. Rest is the underlying force above which everything else moves around. Those who believe indifference to be the root of evil believe man's will triumphs nature's— an ambitious claim to say the least.

Taking this into the human realm, action is only required to combat that which we perceive as the negative, which furthers the cycle of negation, thus counteracting nature's indifference to morals. Most human actions, especially today, are carried out with thoughtless vanity.

Higher spirituality is naturally moral through its inhuman amorality. Its goodness is expressed through stillness and inaction rather than constant reaction and response. This reflects itself in the cycle of karma, which is determined by cause and effect. Those who exit karmic samsara are, however, freed from this cycle.

Turning the tables now, imagine a person with the worst luck imaginable. They are, statistically speaking, an anomaly. They are an extremely small percentage of the human population. Throughout their years, they've been stomped on, abused, held back and forced by unfortunate encounters with malicious beings into a mental space of unfathomable darkness. To an outsider, their life may appear unendurable.

This person— in this particular scenario choosing life over death— develops their own adjusted way of navigating the world. From nature's point of view, such a worldview can be seen as a mutation. If we base knowledge in experience, we wouldn't expect an average joe to navigate the world with the same nuanced web of beliefs as our theoretical Supreme Sufferer.

In other words, those who have been subject to extreme negativity at the hands of others often end up behaving in very strange ways— a reaction. That doesn't mean that all strange people are victims or survivors. But many victims and survivors end up finding strength in differentiation. Their lives become ripples of this differentiation, in the same way that their abusers' lives are irrevocable ripples of hatred and malice. The act of resisting the darkness becomes the sufferer's identity, thus perpetuating the darkness even further. This is when people start saying that it is, "impossible to ever get over something."

Most of us experience this to some degree. We respond to the negative circumstances in life— fear, scarcity, anger— with a deep internal response rather than letting things just wash over us. In doing so, we charge these experiences with reactive energy and allow them to steer us away from the path of benevolent indifference, the path of nature. We often push the snowball of that which makes us suffer into motion instead of leaving it alone.

Evil is not the foundation of life. The problem is that spontaneous mutative negativity infects human psyches in the way that viruses and parasites (negating forces within nature) infect organisms. They cause people to react, and through reaction comes artificiality and unnecessary human intervention. The cycle thus continues. Only through exiting it do we find peace.

We can resist the infection by being naturally kind, calm, and compassionate. This is a choice. You can choose to arbitrarily hate whatever you want, but that is a generative choice, not the default. You can choose to react to anything you like or dislike, but doing so merely sets a process in motion that will eventually be out of your control, and thus an unnecessary potential threat. Our default mode of functioning, should we choose to cultivate it, is calmness and indifference. It's neither blatant evil nor blatant good. In letting darkness wash over us just like anything else, we allow nature to neutralize it just as it does everything else.

Disrupt Yourself

"Technology is destructive only in the hands of people who do not realize that they are one and the same process as the universe."
— Alan Watts

Tech people like to talk about disruption. How disruptive is a business? How is someone 'shaking up' an industry? This is an attempt at being progressive through business, which never works quite as anyone plans. Shaking things up is seen as an opportunity for profit rather than some sort of genuinely constructive thing. If anything, this is a destructive pattern that creates value only where something new is created. In this sense, disruption might make money, but in a strange way it fractures systems. It pushes them towards dissolution in the way that hitting a brick wall with a hammer eventually makes the wall fall down.

In this sense, disruption in the external world functions much like attachment does. When we try to disrupt the world as it functions, we overestimate our place within it. This is pure ego, which is why it is so prominent in the overzealous world of technology . But what happens if, as meditation teaches us to direct our attention inward, we direct our desire to disrupt things inward? What happens if we stir the pot of the self rather than trying to cause a sir in the world?

Incredibly transformative things happen, usually. Why? Most of us are extremely stubborn. Challenge someone's motives or try to ask them deep questions about why they do what they do and they will often become hostile. *Why are you questioning me? How dare you? Are you being condescending?* The little ego monster in each of us wants to badly to never be wrong about anything. This ego is similarly responsible for the impulse to try to shake up the external world. When we start questioning ourselves, though, walls of insecurities and ego blocks come tumbling down. These are the very walls that keep you shielded from reality, from understanding who you actually are. If you are thoroughly entrenched in false reality, disrupting your own system can be dangerous. You might have to make some overhauls.

People spend so much time projecting false assumptions and misunderstandings of the self onto the world. This is an immense amount of wasted energy. When we redirect this energy onto the self, we become actual agents of change rather than just perceived agents of change. You have the most power over yourself, not the world. The way you treat yourself and reflect can completely alter the way you encounter the world.

Lead Invisibly

"A leader is best
When people barely know he exists
Of a good leader, who talks little,
When his work is done, his aim fulfilled,
They will say, "We did this ourselves."
— Lao Tzu, Tao Te Ching

I try to avoid outright politics in these posts for obvious reasons. I know I have followers on both the left and the right. I love that, and I wouldn't want to sacrifice readers on either side for the sake of petty partisan biases. Still, this passage from the Tao Te Ching is always floating around in the back of my mind. We're gonna talk about it. In this passage Lao Tzu fuels a potent critique of modernity. We live at a time in which images and materials rule over any sort of spiritual or moral calculus rooted in nature. These ancient words afford an opportunity for us not to put forth any sort of replacement for this cancerous industrial thinking; that would be foolishly idealistic. But in recognizing what exactly fuels the perpetuation of falsehood in culture, we can over time hope to recognize some sort of alternative for ourselves.

Image culture is, on the surface, all we have left of culture today. The unifications of the past have faded away with the advent of the internet. All boundaries have become blurred. This is both a blessing and a curse. It allows people access to more information and potential knowledge than ever before. But one thing is for sure— humans consume more images today than ever before. Drastically more.

On the level of basic consciousness, this influences even those who don't see themselves as participating in such a culture. We're all on our screens 24/7; it doesn't matter if you're reading a scientific peer-review journal or *17 Pics Of Celebs That Look Like Bunnies*. We equate images with reality since a large number of people today spend more time focused on images than on reality. When a population is heavily focused on images, the depth of its values fades away. Love becomes all about sex. Identity becomes all about fashion. Truth becomes all about statistics. The observable world becomes exclusively that— observable. People begin to equate their individual experience with the absolute truth. In classic human fashion, they begin to make others suffer for that truth, even if it has no basis in natural reality. Our politics is one of personalized imagery and surface-level opinion.

The gist of this is that we've lost contact with nature. It doesn't take a luddite to see this; the farther we travel into the realm of technological consciousness, the farther we drift away from the real. Technology mirrors human desire. We created what is now creating us in our own self-involved image, not nature's image. And it's spoiled us. It's created an imagistic culture that operates in complex ways despite only serving to gratify our basest impulses. Porn is more popular than ever. Opioid use is more popular than ever. Memes are more popular than ever. A leader advances his or herself by catering to these images, disseminating memes, and inventing ideas of leadership rooted not in reality but in the hearts and minds of the image-obsessed masses.

A lot of people are so caught up in this cycle that they haven't taken any time to reflect on their true feelings. Most importantly, the more time we spend obsessing over image culture and petty identity politics, the less energy we have to devote to the real life practice of everyday life. I watched a war film with my friend the other night, and his response to the film was, "Wow. This really makes me grateful just to be able to go to work everyday." That just made me sad. Our forefathers died so we could be grateful to spend 8 hours a day in front of a computer screen?

We all have a remarkable opportunity every day, not to embody our images or false ideals but to instead live out an inborn immutable truth. You're born who you are. Culture tries to change you and force you to buy various hats. It will try to convince you that who you are is different from who you naturally are. But you only truly learn about yourself through reflection. The wisdom you require is already within you if you have some time to just sit and listen. If everyone took the time they spend watching the news, reading depthless articles and having depthless conversations, and applied it to looking within, we would all be more peaceful. I don't expect that many people to have the discipline or desire to do this, but those who do implicitly become the leaders in their own worlds and communities, and, by proxy, the world.

Every word spent speaking mindlessly about the leadership of another person is effort wasted, effort that could be directed towards oneself. Follow Lao Tzu's advice. Lay low. Build your own castle of virtue with diligence and, please, keep quiet about it. Treat others with respect. Treat yourself with respect. Don't indulge in vices, images and false desires. Instead of conditioning yourself to be controlled, control yourself. Your example will help others do the same.

As It Is

"However insistently the blind may deny the existence of the sun, they cannot annihilate it."
— D.T. Suzuki

Zen teaches us that a life of pure calm exists should we choose to access it. There is a rock-solid spiritual core that can be known by anyone with the proper tools of self-knowledge and reflection. Your innate spiritual wisdom is uncovered during meditation. The external self is forgotten and a deep wellspring of inner knowledge is accessed. I call this natural wisdom. It cannot be acquired; it is instead uncovered. Just because the calm exists within you and is determined by you does not mean that 'out there' isn't chaotic and crazy. This is a mistake I made for a while in my understanding of meditation. I thought that somehow changing my thinking would change the world.

The fact of that matter is that changing your thinking doesn't ever change the fact of natural wisdom. It doesn't change the world, either. Humans think they are changing the world when all they are doing is changing their relationships to other humans. Changing your thinking simply changes your reaction to the world. If you try to force the world to change, or even to force yourself to acknowledge the facts of the world through a new lens of subjective delusion, you will remain stuck in a mental trap.

This was a crucial realization for me. The world is often outrageous and insane. Nature knows no morals and humans are always changing theirs to fit the tides of historical back-and-forth. What is best for us in the long run rarely appears to be best for us in the short run, and vice-versa. Everyone's always fighting over things like this. Good and evil and everything in between are floating around always. The world is as it is. It is as it has been. It existed before you and will continue to exist after you. Eventually, all life and matter will cease to be. This is the external world. As long as you remain alive, your internal world can connect with the infinitude of the external world.

This is where inner-wisdom comes in. Cultivating it brings you closer to the world as it is rather than you forcing yourself upon the world in an attempt to project a false reality onto it. The lesson of true reflection is that it can't be anything other than what it is. Peace arises when we stop trying to change everything all the time and can simply be.

Living with Awe

Early this morning my cat Rufus was waiting outside my door for me. He used to do this because he wanted food, but since we gave him an unlimited feeder he has no excuse to beg anymore. Now he hangs around when he wants pats, which I love. Instead of getting straight to writing, which is how I usually spend the initial hours of the morning, I spent a solid 20 minutes sitting with Rufus on my lap. I just sat there and pet him; I had his full attention so I figured it only right that he have mine as well.

This sounds very simple, and of course it is. Maybe it was the lucidity of the AM hours, but I felt myself really paying attention to the act of petting my cat. It's these small simple actions and experiences that make up most of our free time, and yet they are so often the things we bias ourselves against as requiring the least attention. After all, petting Rufus could have been a mindless activity that I did while I worried about other stuff or sat on my computer. Instead, I tried making the most of it, and it was deeply rewarding. Oftentimes, living the good life is as simple as paying attention.

Since I first began meditating, I've found this mental switch that turns itself on throughout the day and jolts me into a state of intense awareness. It hit with a particular clarity while petting the cat, but it happens fairly regularly these days. When it does happen, it's truly remarkable, as if a veil has been lifted.

I believe that this heightened awareness can be accessed by anyone who wishes to train themselves to turn on the switch. The more I train myself, the more profound and wonderful these experiences of minutiae are. There's an old story about JRR Tolkien, that people got annoyed when they accompanied him for walks in the forest because he would stop for prolonged periods and simply gaze at a flower, a tree, or a patch of moss. This is the mindful brain at work. If we can easily see everything as a burden, why not just see everything as a miracle instead?

Mindfulness reveals a beautiful world that is scarcely noticed by the distracted mind. Focusing on silence, darkness, and emptiness for a certain amount of time each day returns us to a blank slate from which we can experience the world anew, like a child. Petting my cat this morning felt like a really special experience. You might say, "Jeez, this guy is a crazy sentimentalist." And I accept that assessment from those who haven't yet experienced the mindful attention to detail that comes from really zoning in on the task at hand.

For those of you who have worked towards heightened states of awareness through your mindfulness practice, I encourage you to see how often you can turn the switch on throughout your day. Don't force it, of course, since that defeats the whole purpose. But there are so many opportunities to express awareness every day: cooking, making coffee, listening to someone speak, sitting in the park, art, practicing instruments, doing busywork, reading, love, fixing things, etc.

The principle here that's most important to elucidate is that of inwardness. In looking inside ourselves, we develop a capacity for reflection that grows and becomes more comprehensive and awe-inspiring over time. It plainly and simply makes life more lucid. It allows us to both perceive darkness more objectively and perceive lightness and beauty with an endless sense of curiosity. This is developed from within. It makes even the most boring facets of life interesting again. And it means that we have an entirely new opportunity to navigate life without trying to find this inwardness outside of ourselves.

Mindfulness makes outward seeking less necessary; no need for drugs, dumb entertainment, meaningless sex, etc, to fill the void. You can do those things if you want, but of course what brings you long lasting satisfaction is not the outward seeking of temporary pleasures but the inward cultivation of bliss. Sometimes it takes abstinence from indulgences to recognize the beauty of simplicity. We don't have to become ascetics, but we can reorient ourselves to experience the world with a more attentive set of eyes.

There is Only Change

Think of how many troubles you cause yourself by wanting things to stay the same. People cling to idealized notions of the past and future on all sides of debate, both internally and externally. The secret is that all of this clinging to ideas is false. Every time you idealize the past or future, you neglect the present. Within the present is all there is: the solution to every concern, the perfect infinitude of balance. Similarly, every time you cling to concepts, you deny reality. Concepts exist below reality, as shallow interpretations of that which cannot be conveyed. True reality is inconceivable. This is why we try so hard to pin it down. Lo and behold, there will be no pinning down of reality! And that's ok.

You need not try to force change because it's the only way. Every moment is a brief glimpse of flux from one state to another. You are in a perpetual state of transition from this to that, that to this. When you exist within this balance and understand yourself to be a reflection of the universe rather than an agent of alteration within it, you find an endless reservoir of peace. People who have had near death experiences report this sort of sudden realization of the confluence of moments, the deep nature of awareness. Without the burden of thought or judgment, and without the clinging to life that scares us away from life itself, you find clarity of mind. Every moment is a different form of adaptation. People consider some days good and others bad. While you're at a wedding, someone else is at a funeral. This is so obvious that we forget it all day every day. Each moment is a blessing with the proper point of view.

Expectations vary based on knowledge; disappointments and victories vary based on expectations. The relationship between what we think will happen and what happens is always tenuous, always being brought into question. Despite this, people foolishly try to plan exactly what will happen. This provides a certain illusion of security. The truth of the matter is that there's no security. Your life could flip itself upside down at any moment, and guess what? It's still your life. Through all external changes you continue to exist for the duration of your life. Better to cultivate the skills needed to adapt to change and chaos rather than taking refuge in the false security of ignorance, or idealizing non-reality.

Be Still

"The righteous man is righteous still in any place and any company, and the unrighteous man is unrighteous." —Meister Eckhart

Nature teaches the ideal of strength in stillness. A tree with many years of growth and cultivation behind it is stronger than a young flimsy thing. Its roots go deeper. The old tree has weathered endless storms, soaked up the resulting water and used it to fortify itself, remaining still, stolid and strong. It moves slightly in the wind, but this movement decreases until it reaches its peak size. Unexpected lightning strikes or lumber crews notwithstanding, the strong tree sticks around for a long time.

That which is weathered and aged is strong. That which is pliable and young, while often full of hope and potential, is still weak and vulnerable. With wisdom and age comes strength and stillness. Modern society shed its ancient human respect for elders as part of its ethos of newness and progression, which is a shame, really. With age comes the wisdom of experience— the only true wisdom there is. The tree is at its strongest right before it begins to wither and decay. The end of the growth stage is the strongest part of that stage and thus the entire life cycle. We write off the opinions of our elders as "from another time", but there is no other time! We must re-learn to cherish the wisdom of time.

Nature teaches us that size and profundity are reflected in stillness. The vastness of space, the whole of a mountain, the massive peak-growth tree— these all appear massive and unmoving to the diminutive human. There's an important lesson here, one of the many lessons to be learned through simple observation. Strength lies not in action, reaction, offense or defense, but in stillness. He who weathers the storm beats the storm; fighting the store is futile. Too many people get caught up in the storm. People let small unfavorable events set off chain reactions that lead to cataclysmic faults. Sometimes these events snowball out of control so quickly that by the time one has recognized them and returned to the senses, it's too late. Over time, some people learn from the destructive nature of reaction; they acquire vital knowledge of the nuance of cause-and-effect. They grow cautious. And they slow down. They act mindfully and slowly rather than hastily and thoughtlessly.

There's great wisdom in silence and great profundity in stillness, precisely because most people today are so unaccustomed to these qualities. The person who embodies the strength of stillness is less common now than at any other point in history, and therefore extremely important. The world is hurdling towards a mindless abyss of its own design. In its push, humanity has forgotten what it means to operate within nature, respect it, and learn from it. People look down on nature, believing themselves to have conquered it just because they live in cities and can farm organic vegetables on their rooftops. This is completely missing the point. Immersion in the inhuman teaches us the limits of human arrogance. The secret to regaining control over ourselves is to recognize our supreme powerlessness and to respect the universe.

Through stillness, we find the strength that leads to peace. People are mistaken about peace. They think it comes from the very qualities of youth I mentioned earlier— pliability, flexibility, and softness. Rather, peace comes when we close our mouths, close our eyes, and reflect. It doesn't come through youthful exuberance, defensiveness and ephemerality. It is the giant tree, unflinching in the face of struggle after years and years of torment and conditioning. Oddly, peace requires a lot of suffering, at least on the personal level. If we listened to our elders, we would know this.

Discover the Moment

"The human situation is seen for what it is—a quenching of thirst with salt water, a pursuit of goals which simply require the pursuit of other goals, a clutching of objects which the swift course of time renders as insubstantial as mist."
—Alan Watts

"Eating rice isn't preparation for shitting; shitting isn't preparation for making manure. And yet these days people think that high school is preparation for college and college is preparation for a good job."
—Kodo Sawaki

The lives of many people reflect the life cycle of a tabloid newspaper, perpetually revolving around the Next Big Thing. The stuff of the past is swiftly forgotten; the stuff of today is but fodder for the future. Let's take a second and review some deeply ingrained memories of conditioning. What sort of questions are we asked by society-at-large? These are what immediately come to mind for me:

What comes next? What is this moment leading up to? What are you going to do with your life? Who do you want to be when you grow up? How will you get there?

These are the questions we're asked often as young people and as we grow up they stick with us, perhaps because they're rather traumatic questions on a spiritual level. From an impressionable age we're encouraged to always be looking ahead, to the point that some young people end up planning their lives decades in advance. Eventually they hit retirement age and have to find things to do in the present, with no preparation for the Next Big Thing. This causes people a great deal of distress.

There are equally as many questions that young and old people alike don't hear (or perhaps that we ignore):

What matters right now? What are you grateful for? What would you do with your life if money didn't matter? Who were you before you started trying to be somebody? Why do you do the things you do?

And, my favorite— drum roll, please:

If you walked outside right now and were hit by a truck, would your loved ones celebrate your life?

These are the real questions. It's important to give yourself the tough love that others might not give you for lack of confidence. I lost one of my best friends at 22. He was a few months away from graduating college— I recall this being a very important point of discussion after he died. At his funeral, the primary topic of detached eulogistic preaching was a perceived sense of wasted opportunity. His loved ones were disappointed that they didn't get to see him do all of this stuff they had been grooming him for: graduate college, get a good job, get married, have children, etc.

This eclipsed their expression of gratitude for past memories, since the reality of the situation was rather grim and they were often at odds in daily life. People rely on future projections to keep them shielded from the potentially discomforting truth of the present. But when someone has serious trouble and isn't getting the support they need, the future stuff doesn't matter. It's thin ice at that point; eventually it breaks.

I tell this story not to bum you out but because I think about my friend every day. His presence in my life as a memory influences my practice and fortifies the strength in my belief that today is all we have. This moment is the most important moment. We hear that statement a lot but do we really internalize it? I don't think so. As I write this, I'm unexpectedly tearing up with simple gratitude for life. Sometimes tragedy enters the picture and reminds us of everything we do have. It's easy to take the essence of life for granted when we become mindless and distracted. Once we're brought back to reality, the true emotions come to the surface. We really do want to be here. Life is precious.

I ask you not to make some sort of revolutionary change in your life all of the sudden but to use your proclivity for mindfulness practice to focus more on the present. Today is not preparation for something else. It's all we have. If you make it as fruitful and beautiful as you can, you can expect a fulfilling tomorrow.

Meditation and the Hedonic Treadmill

"I might have added, as it entered my mind to do, that some people found satisfaction in being. Being. Others were taken up with becoming. Being people have all the breaks. Becoming people are very unlucky, always in a tizzy. The Becoming people are always having to make explanations or offer justifications to the Being people."
— Saul Bellow, Henderson the Rain King

What is happiness and why do we chase it like rabid dogs? To put this question in perspective, let's consider the idea of the hedonic treadmill. This concept is defined simply as, *"...the observed tendency of humans to quickly return to a relatively stable level of happiness despite major positive or negative events or life changes."* The implications of this are huge. Obvious as they seem, why don't we learn from them? Because with our greatest strength (adaptation) comes our greatest weakness (insecurity).

The transformation of the mind that occurs during meditation confirms this idea that happiness is static. One of our greatest strengths as humans is that we adapt. The cost of this flexibility is that we sometimes lose sight of our own ability to adapt.

We convince ourselves that we need more and more of this or that to be happy when in reality we already have the secret. The secret is to simply exist.

What, then, optimizes happiness? Not grubbing at the future, the shiniest things, or the glitz and glamor. What optimizes happiness and contentment is making sure your hardware is functioning properly. Exercise, meditation, learning, love, good conversation, healthy foods, sleep, meaningful work—these are the elements that make up an existence optimized for contentment rather than clinging.

Why did I choose these particular activities? They come from within and rely on an integration of our essential humanity with the world at large. They connect us rather than separate us. They remind us of the web of nuanced interrelations that makes up the world. The activities that make us miserable are activities that hand our contentment over to— overworking, clinging, addiction, wealth, fame— in exchange for a 'brighter future'. Those who do this eventually find that such a future never comes, just more adaptation. We trade control of ourselves for these methods of feeling we have acquired the world, but the world cannot be acquired. When we return to activities that are fundamentally tied in with meaningful existence, we find what we are looking for. Part of this comes from not looking so hard. Who wants to pet the rabid dog?

In this sense, the less you need, the more you have. If our strength is in adaptation, we should not see this as an opportunity to pillage worldly pleasures for all they are worth. Instead, we should see it as a warning sign. If one attaches oneself to acquisition and attachment, there will never be enough. The mind may try to convince itself otherwise, because that's its job— to adapt. Our power as humans comes from our ability to transcend this, to step off the treadmill and take a stroll through reality.

Enjoy Your Problems

"The most important point is to accept yourself and stand on your own two feet. Enjoy your problems." — Shunryu Suzuki

When I first found this line by Suzuki, I thought it was silly. Enjoy your problems? Easy for a master to say! How can normal people with everyday responsibilities enjoy their problems? And yet these words resonate more with me every day as my practice grows and my life experience increases.

Life is full of 'problems'. Seeing them as problems turns life itself into a problem. What is a problem for one person is no problem for another. In other words, most of what we call 'problems' are really just made up perspectives on events. The meditating mind is more honest about this process. It doesn't discriminate good from bad, but simply lets everything come and go. When we do this in a controlled way during meditation, the same mindset eventually carries over into everyday life.

The people I admire most are those who do not shy away from difficulties, but instead dive in. They welcome challenges, recognizing them not as inconveniences but as the very fabric of life, a chance to grow and evolve. I like to see this as following the way of nature. When we exist in a vacuum and avoid risks and uncertainties, we ignore nature. Whenever humans ignore nature, they are punished. But when we acknowledge existence as a constant state of flux and chaos, we don't view problems as problems. They become opportunities. Even the smallest disturbances are chances to be mindful, to retain composure and not have emotional outbursts.

With an increased capacity for survival comes an inability to recognize our blessings. Modern people are like this. We're so comfortable that we don't realize what we've got. We're blessed with health, comfort and knowledge; we should work hard each day to use it to the utmost. Not to do so is, again, to go against nature. Will you open yourself to growth and reflection or let yourself stagnate?

Slow & Steady

"He who rules men lives in confusion;
He who is ruled by men lives in sorrow.
Yao therefore desired
Neither to influence others
Nor to be influenced by them.
The way to get clear of confusion
And free of sorrow
Is to live with Tao
In the land of the great Void."
—Chuang Tzu

The "get rich and famous really quick" narratives of popular culture were accompanied by equally crazy and Dionysian narratives of people completely burning out. Alongside the trope of the young genial celebrity came the trope of the tortured young star. The popular narratives weren't that these people were exploited by a ridiculously inhuman machine of culture, but that they were too brilliant for this planet. What a convenient story to cover up this false modern paradigm of what constitutes "greatness".

Next, we have the sales pitch of "lose X pounds in X days!" "save the planet!" "get what you want now!" and "real life shouldn't take any work!" These narratives are just as harmful as the commercial exploitation of artists as tragic figures, if not more-so, since they directly impact all of us. These narratives function sort-of like pornography— they make us think that something nuanced and beautiful is rote and mechanical. Life is mysterious and worth living; the industrial conception of life as a robotic material game is not.

Nothing good is done quickly. Plain and simple. Every day everyone on this planet wakes up and does their thing. Circumstances vary as vastly as appearances and biological predispositions. We are all very different. But if we train ourselves to return to the mysterious slow-and-steady narratives of nature rather than the hastily inorganic clear-cut narratives of culture, we find incredible strength.

The truth of the matter is that people have been less optimized for slow and steady than we have for fast and chaotic— the twist is that fast and chaotic appeals to us as an image in our collective malaise. We're comfortable. We don't take many risks. We're kept living in a certain degree of fear of the unknown. Our aversion to the unfamiliar is natural, but it's heightened by fake narratives.

It's precisely the thought that we can accomplish great things quickly that makes doing so nearly impossible for most people today. The person who accomplishes great things doesn't louse around and live vicariously through cultural narrative. They treat every day as an opportunity. Instead of wallowing, they do stuff, even if it's just chores around the house. Instead of complaining, they work on themselves. Every tiny action is an opportunity rather than a burden: eating is a chance to be healthier and more energetic. Physical activity is a chance to connect mind and body. Meditation is a chance to get to know yourself better. Problems that arise are the fuel for this attitude; they are opportunities to learn something new. Life is a struggle for all, but it can be a positive struggle if we learn to spiritually reconfigure ourselves towards self-respect, sincere reflection, and constructive action.

The idea that we've been stubbornly taught is that this is about progress. We want to progress as people in the same way we want society to progress. But where is society progressing? Off a cliff, if you refer to any basic stat sheet. And so here's the crux of the matter: we don't learn mindfulness to progress. We learn it to make the most if what we already have. Everything we need is right here. All the stuff humans need has always been right here. We have forced this idea that we have to always be growing and changing into the Next Thing, all the while everyone seems to be neglecting what they've already been given. We're applied the planned obsolescence purportedly reserved for consumer products to ourselves. Work with what you've got, slowly and steadily. Treat each day as an opportunity to be grateful. The slow-and-steady race requires a journey inward rather than outward.

Escape the Wormhole

Sometimes in my leisure reading I get sucked down an informational or political wormhole. I've heard people justify this by saying that humans are political creatures, but I don't think humans are specifically political creatures any more than they are specifically religious, economic, or biological creatures. These are just labels. We are all of them at once. I think humans are drawn to ideas about these topics because delusions help people get through the day.

Vapid political concepts and ideological posturing give people the illusion that their lives have meaning. Spending even an hour reading political stuff is like putting a weirdly comfortable hat on when you then go outside after— it causes you to see the world through a lens that is not your own. Over time people forget about the lens and simply believe that what they see is the truth. This is where things get dangerous. This is the lens of ideology. It clouds your vision whenever you stop being honest with yourself or try to adopt an external worldview. The lens relies on your critical thinking ability and intelligence, but then subverts those qualities to its own ends. When you think from the point of view of an -ism, you lose the ability to think for yourself. This is the wormhole. It just keeps going.

For this reason I think it's important to cultivate all sides of any debate in one's head. This is initially frustrating. Everyone makes false assumptions, since most political positions are temporary positions and do not reflect the deeper realities of the world. I've learned to look to nature for my politics in the same way I look to it for my religion. Nature balances creation and destruction. It functions in accordance with a mysterious hierarchy of processes. It is what it is, and so it can't be questioned. It is the "nameless name", as Lao Tzu said of the Tao. In nature, there are no petty human morals. There is no forced conception of goodness or justice outside of what exists. The deep structure of things operates in such a way that everything works itself out in time.

Writing this, I realize that this is a perspective I have always had, beneath all the trying on of various hats. I feel I was born with it, having grown up in the woods faithful in the strength of nature. These ideas can't be acquired through other humans; they must simply be observed. When you approach ideas from your inborn perspective rather than an acquired perspective, you pick up important inconsistencies. You can be perfectly honest. You can trust yourself. This trust prevents your ideas from being flimsy or ephemeral.

The problem with wormholes, on the other hand, is that they are often very flimsy. People can talk the talk of an ideology that two weeks ago they didn't even know existed. College students do this with radicalism. Dejected middle-aged white people do this with Buddhism. What truly astonishes me is the lack of perspective some people seem to have. Putting on the cloak of ideology is not a symptom of who you are, but who you think you are. Years later, those who are too quick to adopt ideas without questioning them will look back and think, "How foolish I was."

All it takes to reverse the process of the wormhole is to consciously decide to turn it around. Meditation helps with this since it lets you access your inborn morality and sense of truth. Over time, what you think is true fades away and what is actually true emerges. You'd be shocked how long you've been conditioned to believe certain things that are completely ungrounded in reality. I find this process of the rediscovery of the true self to be invigorating, albeit sometimes overwhelming. Regardless, it's better than the wormhole. It lets us see life for what it is, and act accordingly.

Ride the Energy Wave

I always know nature will provide me with salient metaphors for living. I spent a day last weekend swimming off the coast of Massachusetts with my girlfriend and was reminded of this. Humans are drawn to beaches and oceans specifically for a reason. Oceans are appealing. They are consistent. Their vastness provides us with a sense of serenity, humility, and comfort. Within the water itself, we float in between states, neither standing firmly on earth nor flying through the air. Psychoanalysts believe that humans are drawn to water because floating in its ether can be likened to floating in the womb. We yearn for the security and beauty of the sea as a godly motherly figure. To float is to exist beyond duality, to be neither one thing nor another. It's also really fun.

It only makes sense, then, that the mysterious inner and outer workings of the ocean can provide us with some valuable metaphors for living. Personally, I am drawn particularly to the meditative crash of ocean waves. I love the sound. I love the way the waves beat up against me when they hit. I love the sheer consistency and strength of them. No wave is ever the same as the wave that came before it, but it always arrives. Its energy flows, peaks, and then washes ashore. The cycle repeats itself endlessly. It's reliable and guaranteed; this is the way nature functions.

There are times that we experience waves of energy. This energy could come from some sort of hormonal harmony or internal feeling of balance. It could come from quitting bad habits, starting good habits, falling in love, achieving something you've worked hard for, or overcoming adversity. It could just come out of nowhere. These waves flow consistently. They are the way of nature. No matter how down in the dumps a person thinks they are, there are always energy waves. Some people recognize them and ride them, while others are distracted and let them go by.

When you assume an attitude of scarcity and attachment, you might not recognize these waves when they come along. They can even bash into you and knock you over if you aren't prepared for them. This is what happens when people who have internalized destructive thought patterns experience things they should be grateful for— they miss them. It's possible to be so engrossed by your own self-indulgent negativity that you don't recognize when opportunities or even simple pleasures come along. In the same way that debt often creates more debt and bogs people down, an imbalance of thoughts pushes you in the direction you devote the most attention to.

Some people never learn how to pay attention to the waves. They get knocked down again and again simply because they have not figured out that they can attune their attention and prepare for the waves. Eventually, though, usually with age and maturity, most people figure out ways to deal with these tides. Some do this better than others. Those who do it best consciously work to cultivate their attention. They remain mindful at all times, lest they miss a distant swell that could develop into a wave. When these waves do come along, and you're prepared for them, they push you into the beautifully consistent rhythm of life. Learning to prepare yourself for the swell and the crash helps you remain versatile and consistent. In moulding yourself to work with the current rather than against it, you come to resemble the water yourself. Bruce Lee had a whole thing about this,

"You must be shapeless, formless, like water. When you pour water in a cup, it becomes the cup. When you pour water in a bottle, it becomes the bottle. When you pour water in a teapot, it becomes the teapot. Water can drip and it can crash. Become like water my friend."

When you learn to ride the waves of energy that inevitably come at you, you put other pieces of the puzzle into place.

Discovering Beginner's Mind

Sometimes I sit down for my daily meditation practice and, well, I take it for granted. I forget the proper posture, or the proper breath. I fidget. My mind wanders and I let it dwell on various thoughts despite having the ability to control it. This is what happens when Zazen becomes "second nature"— we get too used to it. In getting used to it, it sometimes becomes difficult to remember how to assume the position of Beginner's Mind.

What is Beginner's Mind? It's so simple that it often feels difficult to properly grasp. The great master Suzuki said, "In the beginner's mind there are many possibilities, but in the expert's there are few." When we are new to something, we approach it without the mental baggage that is accrued as we get used to it. It is crucial in Zen to retain Beginner's Mind so that we don't fall into laziness in our practice and, by extension, life. The trap of Expert's Mind is that it comes with heightened responsibility. If we don't assume that responsibility we lose sight of the path. We must remain mindful of Beginner's Mind and not to let our 'knowledge' about meditation or Zen get in the way, no matter how 'far along' in this endless journey we are.

I still have memories of my very first meditation sessions when I was 13 and 14. I realize now that some of the most profound illuminations I've ever experienced emerged from this state of pure naïveté, but these states of 'samadhi' still surprise me today, at least a few times per week. This internal knowledge and wisdom builds over time and, compounded, is incredibly valuable, but it means nothing if we forget the true simplicity of the practice itself We must remember that insight is available in every moment. We are never building towards it; we are simply figuring out how to break down the mental barriers between us and it. That's why it surprises us at the least expected times.

The key, as Suzuki reminded everyone again and again, is to retain the proper posture and breath in Zazen and to practice everyday. The simplest elements of the practice are the most important. If you focus too much on the complexities and details of Expert's Mind, you will forget the more crucial simple details. Even if you sit every day and do your best to live mindfully, you will at times fall victim to mindless habits. In a strange sense, being aware of this victimization makes 'the fall' that much more difficult to recover from. Not to fear, though. The gift of mindfulness is the ability to apply our diligence. In remembering the simple state of meditative awareness, these obstacles simply become signposts on the journey.

Do to Know

"Knowing is the fruit of doing." —Bhagavad Gita

In college I was exposed to endless schools of critical thought that were always referred to as "theoretical". In the fogged glass house of the present-day academy, this term may be used with endearment. To me it just connotes a certain arrogance, a highfalutin intellectualism that prevents eager minds from discovering actual truth and instead leaves them with unnecessarily complicated false ideas about how things work. As soon as these students leave the academy, they either forget such theories or apply them in vain, seeing as they have no basis in observable fact nor even spiritual metaphysics.

Some people think that knowledge through experience discounts metaphysics. In fact, the opposite is the case. You are fully convinced and aware of your experience. This isn't rampant individualism as much as it is the belief that what is knowable can only truly be knowable through your own absorption. Teachers can lead you to the depthless water of spiritual teaching, but it's your job to dive in. There is no need to share it or force it upon anyone else.

This is why I find it so fascinating that the staunch individualists of the present era, those who simultaneously believe they have complete agency over themselves and nature but who also subscribe to the very limited materialist dogma of science, are often so vehemently opposed to religion. Honest religious experience is one of the only forms of healthy individualism, usually because true practitioners know to keep their realizations to themselves. The person who wishes to know this universally pervasive super-sensory force we call "God" can take a journey to find it. If one takes this journey in earnest, the results of it will usually have to be kept to oneself. I believe this conception of spiritual truth could help at least a few lost souls in contemporary society find a higher sense of truth and purpose. Through meditation we discover both the follies of religious puritanism and the follies of scientific materialism. Pure consciousness leads the way toward wisdom.

Meditation is so important because it is the cultivation of direct knowledge in experience. Sometimes I like to think of myself as a miner when I meditate. My mind works diligently to focus itself. It knows it might not strike gold or even find any coal, but it chips away, building tunnels and slowly removing debris along the way. We can thank science in this realm— it's used its ample funding and tools to prove that meditation does in fact alter brain chemistry. Through regular meditation, you structurally differentiate yourself from both others and your prior selves. This, coupled with a metaphysical differentiation through the knowledge acquired through meditative experience, is what constitutes the spiritual journey.

Trust Your Body

"He who loves his body as he loves the world can be trusted to govern the world." —Chuang Tzu

People have become disconnected from their bodies. The rise of running, yoga, and other physical practices reflects a general desire among people who wish to correct the mind-body disconnect. These practices have become so popular that they are often seized as business opportunities. Once this happens, they are transformed into tools for productivity and success rather than mindfulness. People quickly lose the point, even if they have good intentions. The secret to mindfulness is to do it for its own sake. When people focus on an activity for the result, they often neglect the essence of the activity. If you focus too intently on a target, you're likely to become shaky and miss. But when you let go, you relax. You allow yourself a degree of objectivity and neutrality. You will find yourself consistently performing well rather than burning out focusing on a pinpoint target.

People perform better this way. This seems counterintuitive but it's not; when you divorce actions from expectations you remain strong and still rather than weak and wavering. This strength comes from letting things flow naturally rather than forcing them. You can become successful by being forceful, but it often comes at a price— peace of mind. With physical activities, strength is built not through obsessing over results but instead through engaging mindfully with the process. You accomplish great feats by doing things one small step at a time. Every rep, step and breath is an opportunity to grow, but should be performed in and of itself. Exercise for its own sake opens up the world of mindfulness. Once you are mindful of your body, you start to feel at home in your own skin.

This feeling of belonging within yourself helps you encounter the world in an entirely new way. Instead of feeling alienated from your body, you feel comfortable. When people feel alienated from their bodies, they feel alienated from the world and encounter constant discomfort. They feel unable to engage properly with the world and experience meaninglessness.

With deliberate action, the meaningfulness of life returns. Making peace with your body means finding peace in the physical world. All of the problems that arise from the physical world– relationships, money, etc— are aided by cultivating physical strength and comfort with your body. Breathe deeply and go one step at a time.

Remove the Unnecessary

"To attain knowledge, add things everyday. To attain wisdom, remove things every day."
— *Lao Tzu*

When we meditate, we recognize thoughts as they come and go. But what exactly happens over time when we become more aware of our thoughts? To put it simply— we begin to audit ourselves. When a business is cooking the books, it usually takes a federal tax audit for them to be taken down. All of the inconsistencies and dishonesties are uncovered, the numbers are adjusted to reality, and the entity collapses under its own weight. It essentially collapses under reality. Meditation has this effect on the ego. All of our sandcastles of false desire, ambition and clinging are washed away. Don't be scared— becoming a regular meditator won't make your life collapse around you like some sort of spiritual form of bankruptcy. The good thing about the inner-life is that it is immaterial and thus cannot collapse.

This is why meditation is so transformative. In auditing your thought patterns and realizing how many inconsistencies and dishonesties there are, the mind automatically begins to correct them on its own. This happens as soon as we let go. It's truly incredible how much fluff we fill our heads with. Thoughts of vanity, attachment, disappointment and anger. When the mind is left unchecked it creates vast storms of chaotic thoughts. It cultivates falsehood, delusion and fantasy. It drives us crazy, basically. Contrary to modern opinions about religion, many of the premodern religious rituals sought merely to quiet the mind. These rituals— prayer, chanting, sacrifice, contemplation, etc— aren't actually about pleasing a God or cultivating good karma, but about quelling the ego, focusing the mind and allowing all of the chaotic dust to settle. Most people have either forgotten or never understood this purpose of such rituals. Meditation revives it. it allows the mind to become centered and clear.

Try to remove something each day. This is a simple enough habit to get into. Maybe it's a destructive habit. Maybe it's a piece of clutter in your apartment. Maybe it's one less drink, one less smoke, one less thought of self-doubt. All that this removal process requires is the cultivation of mindfulness. It gets easier over time. You will be astounded by how much extra energy, time and focus you have once you begin to remove all of the mindless wasteful excess.

Knowledge and Wisdom

"Meditation is not passive sitting in silence. It is sitting in awareness, free from distraction, and realizing the clear understanding that arises from concentration." — Thich Nhat Hanh

As a lifelong reader who meditates every day, I've had no choice but to swallow my pride and acknowledge that some things cannot be learned. What do I mean by this? Many people think of wisdom and knowledge as the same thing. Many educational institutions, scientists, artists and others simply believe that the more knowledge they acquire, the smarter they'll be. People spend lifetimes trying to conquer knowledge at the expense of wisdom. In spending more and more time working with computers, it seems humans have started to believe that they themselves function similarly to computers. The more information they can fit into their heads, the better— or so they think.

A friend recently tried to argue the point that humans today are inherently more wise and more 'valuable' than humans of the past simply because they have more potential access to information. I found myself vehemently disagreeing with this sentiment. Time doesn't objectively make anyone smarter and it certainly doesn't make anyone wiser. Those who choose to access wisdom find it, but throughout history they have always been a small minority. Time may contribute to a larger collective pool of knowledge, but this is not wisdom. Access to this information may give people the appearance of being informed, but it doesn't make them wiser.

This fundamental error comes from people feeling historically unsure of the idea of wisdom. Young people today are not that religious. Religion has been pitted against knowledge and, as always, the popular arguments against religion rarely take into account the valuable wisdom that can be produced by spiritual experience. Even meditators often just start because they think meditation is going to make them calmer and more efficient. A mere century of industrialization and modernization has convinced people that man's highest consciousness is productive consciousness. What an odd paradox that as man moves towards material satisfaction and comfort he finds himself further and further away from spiritual life! There cannot be material satisfaction if the mind is uncalm.

Here's the fundamental difference between knowledge and wisdom— knowledge comes from out there, while wisdom comes from within. To put it simply: knowledge is acquired, wisdom is uncovered. The things that you truly know, not facts or statistics or even things that can be expressed in language, are already in you waiting to be uncovered by your attention. Spiritual experience is the process of recognizing this innate wisdom. Some compassion comes when we recognize that all people have this wisdom and can access it. Sitting and reflecting often requires a certain humility and calmness. When we stand back and give ourselves some respect and some space, wisdom emerges. It comes in the quiet periods after thoughts begin to fade away.

Reconnect with Nature

"We do not "come into" this world; we come out of it, as leaves from a tree. As the ocean "waves," the universe "peoples." Every individual is an expression of the whole realm of nature, a unique action of the total universe." —Alan Watts

I've always loved the works of Alan Watts. For a beginner, his writings and personality entice the mind and draw it further into curiosity. This is integral for those trying to find some sort of foundation in Zen. Many Eastern philosophical concepts are difficult for beginners to grasp. There are countless pop cultural myths about spiritual tradition that require a fair amount of reconditioning to reverse. True understanding takes work. Most importantly, it takes daily meditation.

Today I'd like to take some time to delve into one of Watts' favorite concepts— emergence. It's the simple idea that, instead of being dropped into the world like an alien, we emerge out of the world as an integral expression of it. We're a reflection of it, not a product of it. Your initial reaction to this might be, "Duh," but I think you'll find it interesting to get into.

I find emergence particularly important to think about at this point in history, when man finds himself pitted against nature in a weird technological battle for progress, change, and 'disruption'. Rarely is this credo ever questioned. This represents, for me, the crux of a technological battle against nature. That which is most disruptive is perceived as beneficial, while that which is understated, simple and peaceful is considered obsolete or boring. Serenity is overlooked because it doesn't cause a stir. This is because the cult of progress relies on this concept of man vs. nature. It relies specifically on a false sense of conflict between these two entities that are in reality one and the same. Anything that controls us or holds us back is viewed not as a sacred force to be respected but instead as a challenger to be overcome.

When we feel separate from nature, we begin to feel like aliens. When work becomes about abstracted processes, machinery, numbers and middle-managing, humans feel differently than when work is about respectfully cooperating to accomplish some sort of goal. The further your work is removed from reality, the more prone you are to feeling alienated. Seeing as most people today are not foraging for food, building shelters, or hunting animals, we feel varying degrees of alienation every day. The more we take mere survival for granted, the less we respect nature.

When people feel alienated, they get anxious. They get depressed. They feel wholly responsible for themselves and thus the cult of individuality emerges. This causes internal strife because people are not wholly responsible for themselves. It's not optimal for everyone to think that they can do whatever they want or be whoever they want. Working with nature means working with what you've got and respecting your place, not denying it in favor of some sort of ego projection or fake identity. In recognizing yourself as in-and-of nature rather than as a product of it, you take full responsibility for your circumstances and can be honest with yourself. Trying to find balance and harmony makes life peaceful. Trying to find opportunities to exploit and ways to "change" the world makes life chaotic and artificial.

When nature feels distant and oppositional, people start to think of themselves as gods. They believe that their reality is whatever they decide it is; meanwhile the universe is still operating all around them and through them. The truth exists always, but through a sheer lack of wisdom people put their blinders on and try to force their own truth. This dissonance creates psychological conflict. When we 'return' to nature, we return to our fundamental essence. Like Watts said, we recognize that it is us and we are it. We cannot escape the deep truths of nature. We recognize that maybe barreling forward at any cost is probably not the best way to approach things. In overcoming this sense of natural alienation, we acknowledge that it's OK for things to operate harmoniously. Humans shouldn't attempt to "come out on top" because this is an impossible task. People only feel a need to "disrupt" when they are dissatisfied. To attempt disruption is to attempt to overcome or transcend that of which you are an integral part. This is a life-denying act. There is no escaping nature. Even if Earth becomes uninhabitable and we all blast off into space colonies we're still subject to deep universal laws that we don't truly understand.

This is where I ask you to simplify your life and make peace with nature. Our ancient ancestors understood the importance of this, but we seem to have forgotten it. Being perpetually dissatisfied with your conditions is a choice and leads to constant struggle and egoism. Finding peace, gratitude and solace in simply being alive leads one towards peace, stillness, and natural balance. Personally, I find exercise, hiking and meditation help me connect with nature and respect it. The key is not to challenge nature as a zealous alien warrior, but instead to respect and work gratefully with nature as if a guest or disciple.

Transcending the Dark Side

"To bow to the fact of our life's sorrows and betrayals is to accept them, and from this deep gesture we discover that all life is workable. As we learn to bow, we discover that the heart holds more freedom and compassion than we could imagine." —Jack Kornfield

What happens when you dive into discomfort? In the same way a dark cavern is less scary when you navigate it with a light, exploring your own mind is less difficult when you do so with mindfulness. A lot of people try to uncover the depths of their consciousness without developing mindfulness. They often see things they don't want to see and they let themselves get carried away. Similarly, in meditation we often uncover difficult emotions and ideas. When we sit with them, they become less frightening. The less light you shine on the darkness, the more powerful it remains.

In this respect, we can see meditation as the process by which we shine a light on every thought, good and bad. In observing these thoughts neutrally, we learn that they aren't as terrifying or powerful as we think. Put into perspective, most of our worries can be seen for what they are—relatively insignificant. Part of meditation is recognizing yourself as both the center of the universe and also a tiny ephemeral speck. Making peace with the paradox and the contrast between the two is the work of a meaningful life.

If you indulge in a though, it takes root, and then you need to let go for longer in order to return to no-mind. Sometimes when we meditate thoughts come along that we can't help but grasp onto. The real work of Zen practice is building the inner-strength and stillness to let even the most difficult intrusions go.

What is this process if not the ultimate disempowering of concepts in general? When you reach the point where your greatest fears and insecurities emerge during meditation and no longer cause you harm, you have transcended the mind. You are operating with a script deeper than language. It is the symbolism of intuition and experience. You have conquered these once powerful thoughts through not trying to conquer them. When you let them come, they eventually do go if you don't dwell on them. After you experience this a few times, the darkness is significantly less frightening.

With an acceptance of darkness comes an acceptance of its friends— difficulty, death, confusion, confrontation, dishonesty, among many others. Realizing that the truth isn't so scary if we just try to understand it helps us stop lying to ourselves. It opens up a whole new world of inquiry and awareness. This all inevitably leads toward a more mindful and interesting life.

We're educated our entire lives to trust in the power of mere thoughts. We're taught to worship "thinkers", but at what cost? We're told, "Thoughts and ideas can change the world." Yes, of course they can. Thoughts are the vehicles for many actions. But what happens when the thoughts we don't want to acknowledge come along? If we empower thoughts too much, we become obsessed with the ones that cause us harm, and then they hold us back from true understanding. But when we learn the limits of thought through reflection and experience, we can understand that ideology and mental work must be balanced with direct experience and meditation. A truly holistic self-education is equally mental, physical, and spiritual.

Unwinding the Mind

A lot of people who end up studying meditation do so in response to a negative event in their life. They feel lost and want guidance, and so they seek a path that will redirect them towards their inner-self. I am of the opinion that anything that leads you towards meditation and mindfulness is part of this path. The thing to be careful of is when we start to treat spirituality like a narcotic, or when we use it to try to replace things we once clinged to but have since overcome. This comes from falsely seeing the mind as a possession, something you have, rather than as the substance of your inborn awareness.

The same way good people become evil by clinging to absolute moralities, spirituality becomes unnatural when we attach to it as something "out there". It is not a shoe that you try on and wear around for a while. It's either something you are doing fully or not doing at all. Those who have never read anything about it can access it at any time. Those who are too entrenched in ideas and expectations to practice properly often become disillusioned.

This is why I am weary of talking too much about "how to be Zen", calling yourself by a label or spending money to learn meditation. All of these actions inherently treat the inner-life as something that is acquired from the outside. We don't run around trying to buy blood, skin, hair and other things we already have— why do we try to do this with wisdom? The only way to truly access it is to recognize that it isn't out there. It is inside you waiting to be uncovered.

Understanding this makes meditation significantly easier. Doing things just to do them is easier than doing them for some sort of goal. Meditating to feel good will make you feel bad. Working more to afford more leisure will make you stressed. Being in relationships to feel less lonely will alienate you from yourself. Every time we try to cling to something outside the self for salvation, we invite delusion and falsehood.

At the end of the day, there is only one bit of true spiritual advice: meditate. When you sit and let the dust of your mind settle, you will uncover deep truths. You won't need to think about these truths. In sitting and letting your mind calm itself naturally without thought or judgment, you end up uncovering more wisdom than can be acquired from the outside. Knowledge and information can be amassed in libraries and universities, but self-knowledge is cultivated through reflection. Once we recognize Zen as internal and not external, it ceases to be a real concept. It is more of a process, like wind or snow. It is something that you are doing to yourself through not trying to do it. When we "just sit", we let this mind beyond the mind understand itself better.

Momentary Miracles

"The miracle is not to walk on water. The miracle is to walk on the green earth, dwelling deeply in the present moment and feeling truly alive."
— *Thich Nhat Hanh*

The same mind that is drawn to spirituality is often also drawn to grandeur. We want life to be something greater. We want to achieve our wildest dreams, to meet God, and to have some time to relax along the way. So idealistic! This is why I find Zen to be endlessly fascinating and a lifelong practice; we never quite get it "right", and that's the point. We aren't searching for anything else. We are simply settling into the infinitude of every individual moment.

Zen, practiced over time, reverses the mentality of searching for something else. It reminds us that what we're searching for is already inside each of us. You already have everything you could want or need, but the searching mind can't admit this to itself. The thing that would allow you to feel happy with a billion dollars or 3 kids or a hot bod is already inside you. You're the one making you happy; you simply convince yourself that things outside yourself are catalysts.

Meditation is not about transcendence or achievement. It is about directing your attention inward and noticing things you've never seen before. You realize eventually that the totality of life is simply a collection of all these little thoughts, feelings and experiences. Why should we sacrifice appreciation of them for an abstract obsession with universality? What is a meaningful life if not one lived fully in each tiny moment? Suffering, pleasure, certainty and uncertainty— every feeling and idea on every spectrum is accepted and attended to. No past, no future. Just now.

Every moment is, in this sense, a miracle. It is a miracle insofar as you are able to acknowledge it! In the same way that there is no you without atoms or molecules, there is no life without these tiny moments. Every "boring" activity of the day-to-day is an opportunity for awakening. They are not special moments, but neither is life. Nothing is special, nothing is un-special. The lesson: simply recognizing your experience in the moment is enough to enrich it. At the end of the day, every breath is a gift. When we really internalize this mindset, life completely changes. Activities are not means to other activities. They become purposeful for their own sake. And when this happens, anything can become a beautiful experience. In the words of the Zen masters, "After enlightenment, the laundry!"

Beyond Ideas

"I had a discussion with a great master in Japan, and we were talking about the various people who are working to translate the Zen books into English, and he said, 'That's a waste of time. If you really understand Zen, you can use any book. You could use the Bible. You could use Alice in Wonderland. You could use the dictionary, because the sound of the rain needs no translation."
— Alan Watts

The core lesson of Zen is that we find the real lessons 'outside' of Zen. In other words, Zen encompasses everything but also nothing at all. There are no rules to follow or moral precepts to abide by. There is simply the momentary navigation of the world with an open heart and an aware mind. We don't judge nor do we cling. We simply try to 'tune in' closely to the reality that exists above all concepts and words.

The composer John Cage, an avid Zen practitioner who studied with DT Suzuki, said, "The first question I ask myself when something doesn't seem to be beautiful is why do I think it's not beautiful. And very shortly you discover that there is no reason." Zen's influence on the mind is not what we're used to. It's not, "I believe X and so I will do

X." It is simply an attitude with which we approach the world. It allows us to look closer, find more beauty and create more meaning, not by force but instead by choice.

In this sense, a Zen education is never complete. It is the opposite of the type of education we receive in the professional world. Instead of approaching the world through the lens of history, idealism or materialism, we approach it through a non-conceptual lens, relying on intuition and reflection to guide us. No idea should be spared from your attempt at mindfulness. I have always been an advocate of exposing yourself to as many disparate ideas as you can. This way, you can reconcile all of the strangest conflicting ideas with one another in order to recognize how fragile concepts are. If you only focus on one set of ideas, you end up clinging to them at the expense of others. The fatal result of this is that you misconstrue this limited set of concepts for 'reality' or 'the truth', when it is just a simulation. Ideas are your operating system. The secret is that there is a deeper operating system beneath them, one purely rooted in experience. Experiential knowledge often feels spiritual or intuitive because, like all of reality, we cannot accurately put it into words. This is the deepest wisdom of the spirit and the body. Trying to capture it with words or other types of symbolic expression is a valuable task, but is also sort-of like trying to catch wind in a jar.

Chasing Happiness

"People wear diamond rings on their fingers and think that the fingers feel happy, but actually it is best to wear nothing on the fingers. Fingers feel happy when they forget themselves." —Dogen

People today are obsessed with happiness. Maybe it's our remnant Judeo-Christian values praising "goodness" over all else, or distant fantasies of paradise. Maybe it's a desire to find meaning in a spiritually forgetful world. Maybe it's the false belief that we become happier over time, that we are on a long-term journey towards happiness. We all know deep down that life is not some sort of upward quest towards bliss. It's dynamic and spontaneous; that's what makes it interesting.

Where does this false assumption come from? It comes from feeling dissatisfied. We all feel naturally dissatisfied at regular intervals; it's the way of life. Instead of learning how to make peace with our dissatisfaction, we invent narratives about the past and future that justify our bad feelings in the present and help us cling to a 'better future'. Those who wish to escape the present moment are unhappy. They create ideals, goals, and notions of progression by which those goals can be achieved.

The paradox here is that, if you aren't satisfied in the present moment, no amount of achievement or progress can possibly satisfy you. The present is all we have. When we stake our happiness on an illusory future, we make peace all but unattainable.

This is anything but a hopeless situation. Meditation helps us reorient our attention towards the moment. When we find our salvation in the moment, we don't need to create faraway fantasies. We can simply feel satisfied in being. Isn't this the purpose of life? This is why meditation is the most important activity: it detaches us from results. What convinces us that the diamond rings make our fingers feel happy is just a mental trick. We can feel happy with or without the stimuli once we come to this understanding.

What's crucial is to meditate without the goal of becoming happier. People falsely meditate as an intermediary between themselves and inner-peace. It isn't a bridge towards a new place. You are just settling into where you already are. This is a subtle difference but it encompasses the solution to most of our petty problems and discomforts. You have to stop chasing happiness and just let it come to you.

Quiet the Mind

Buddhism's venerated Four Noble Truths tell us that suffering is caused by attachment. They don't elaborate on the fact that, especially nowadays, most people find deep comfort in day-to-day suffering. We find more ease in suffering than we do in the overcoming of it. The more comfortable people are, the more they prefer the familiar to the unfamiliar. Familiar suffering and mediocrity thus become prioritized over unfamiliar peace and honesty! This is why so many people are filled with the neuroses of fear, guilt and shame.

When we first start sitting, we try letting our thoughts come and go, but we often let the worst hooligans stick around because they're most familiar. *"Ah, hello, drinking too much, it's great to see you. Why don't you stay for a while? Good day, violent anger, I was just thinking about you! Oh and look— another friend, self-loathing, how I missed having you around!"*

Most people who start meditating do so after years of letting layers of delusion and nonsense pile up all around them. Escaping your conditioning is no easy task, especially since it's painted on pretty thick these days. People think they can assume a new personality just by putting on new clothes or talking a different way. We live in extremely materialistic times; people falsely believe that appearances accurately reflect reality. As a result, most cannot distinguish between their genuine motivations and those that have been pounded into them from constant engagement with culture online, in media and in social situations also informed by these inputs.

Here's where it's easy to get overwhelmed. Starting a daily meditation practice seems daunting because, at first, it's not always that comfortable. It's the opposite of materialism— instead of faking and having a bunch of appearances to show for it, we do the real work and have nothing to show for it, because that's the point.

On top of this, psychological stuff appears that you'd rather not deal with. The very impulse that makes materialism so easy for us makes the spiritual peace of meditation feel like a lot of work. Imagine a person sitting in front of you and calmly telling you everything that is inconsistent and delusional in your thinking, as well as everything beautiful and wonderful. Your mind does this to itself during meditation. It doesn't castigate or loathe itself; it just puts all its cards on the table. There's no way to figure this out other than cutting out all the noise and reflecting. It's why meditation changes people's lives; it simply returns them to who they naturally are. As such, we shouldn't approach meditation as a bridge between us and a "better self". You're never becoming better; you are who you are. We simply sit to sit. The true self emerges over time.

Stop Reading This— Go Meditate!

"Feelings come and go like clouds in a windy sky. Conscious breathing is my anchor."
— Thich Nhat Hanh

People today have a strange approach towards real life action. We will do anything to avoid it. We'll read about how to do something to procrastinate from actually doing it! This is a trap; it keeps us so overloaded with information about how to live that we feel paralyzed about actually getting out there and living. Meditation is as simple as sitting cross-legged with your posture straight, closing your eyes, and focusing on your breath. In one, out two. In three, out four. Go to 10 and repeat. There is nothing else. You'll lose your spot. You'll trail off into snowballs of thoughts, good or bad. The key is to always return to the breath. Let the breath be your anchor.

Pretty easy for something so transformative. You'll soon find that it is not as easy as it seems, however. We take our self-conscious minds for granted. We think we can get by without ever reflecting. We think we should optimize for speed rather than reliability. Meditation teaches you just what little control you have over yourself. Realizing this is the first step. After we make peace with it, we can work to continue sitting and regaining control over the mind. Meditation should come first, studying second. Not everyone can have a Zen teacher and so teachers often appear to us in the form of written texts or even personal intuition. Don't be shy to explore books about Zen. Read them but not if they subtract from the time you have to actually practice. This is so simple yet also crucial. Readings only help us understand how to approach meditation. They guide us to the water. It is our job to actually drink the water and internalize the teaching by learning mindfulness ourselves.

That's the real point— mindfulness cannot be transmitted. You are not given it; you already have it and your meditation practice merely helps you uncover it and connect with it. The more consistently you practice, the more mindfulness you uncover. You brush off the dust of everyday life and see a more vibrant world. Just go meditate. No more excuses!

Printed in Great Britain
by Amazon